Backroad Wineries of Northern California

A SCENIC TOUR OF CALIFORNIA'S COUNTRY WINERIES

Written and Photographed by Bill Gleeson

CHRONICLE BOOKS

SAN FRANCISCO

ABOUT THE AUTHOR

Bill Gleeson is a fourth-generation Californian who grew up traveling the back roads of the Central Valley and the gold country. Gleeson's lifelong interest in the roads less-traveled has led to the publication of several other books.

These include a companion book, *Backroad Wineries of Southern California* (1994), as well as the popular *Weekends for Two* series of romantic getaway guides to Northern California, Southern California, and the Pacific Northwest. All are published by Chronicle Books.

A graduate of California State University, Chico, Gleeson lives with his wife, Yvonne, and children, Kari and Jeff, in the Northern California foothills.

All photographs and maps by Bill Gleeson.

Printed in Japan.

Book and cover design: William Reuter Design

Library of Congress Cataloging-in-Publication Data

Gleeson, Bill.
      Backroad wineries of northern California: a scenic tour of California's
      country wineries/by Bill Gleeson.
        p. cm.
      Includes index.
      ISBN 0-8118-0306-6
      1. Wine and wine making—California, Northern. I Title.
   TP557.G58 1994
   641.2'2'097941—dc20   93-4407
                                                              CIP

Distributed in Canada by Raincoast Books,
112 East Third Avenue, Vancouver, B.C. V5T 1C8

10 9 8 7 6 5 4 3 2 1

Chronicle Books
275 Fifth St.
San Francisco, CA 94103

Contents

Introduction

If you've spent a weekend on the much-traveled highways visiting Northern California's most famous wineries, answer this multiple-choice question.

Have you ever:
1. Been stuck in traffic?
2. Felt like you were watching a long tennis match while attempting to cross Highway 29 anywhere between Napa and Calistoga?
3. Fought with a busload of tourists for a smidgen of space along a crowded winery tasting bar?
4. Been herded, sheeplike, through a long, boring, anonymous tour?

If you answered yes to any of the above, it's time to follow the lead of poet Robert Frost and take the road "less traveled by." Only on Northern California's uncrowded back-country wine roads will you meet vintners like Hans Kobler of Lazy Creek Vineyards, who handcrafts small batches of premium wine and pours it for visitors under an ancient walnut tree. In the quiet hills above crowded Napa Valley, you might encounter the friendly descendants of pioneer California vintner Antone Nichelini crushing Cabernet grapes outside the family's antique winery.

A backroad winery tour offers a chance to experience the wine industry in an unhurried, friendly, informal way. At many of the sixty wineries we've featured in the following pages, tastings and tours are led by the owners, who play personal roles in production of their wines. Not only do they tend the tasting bar, but many have responsibility for vineyard maintenance, overseeing the harvest, operating the crusher, and applying labels to bottles.

BACKROAD DISCOVERIES
As you thumb through this book, chances are you'll see some unfamiliar names. Because of the small size and comparatively meager production of the wineries included in these pages, many don't have the retail clout or restaurant distribution channels that the state's large winemaking operations enjoy.

In tiny Deer Park, above St. Helena, for example, winemaker David Clark sells more than 80 percent of his wines to those who visit his stone-walled Deer Park Winery. And while you might find a few bottles of Husch Vineyards wines on the shelves of discriminating wine shops, don't expect to find its La Ribera Cabernet table wine. This popular wine is sold exclusively through the rustic Husch tasting room in Mendocino County.

NOT A CRITIC'S GUIDE
Our criteria for selecting wineries were simple. We skipped over every winery adjacent to any freeway and those set along the well-beaten winery paths of Highway 101, Highway 29, and the Silverado Trail.

While assembling backroad winery guides to Northern and Southern California, we visited scores of small wineries located off the beaten track. In selecting wineries for inclusion, we weren't necessarily guided by wine critics or numbers of county fair awards won. In fact, we passed over a few small establishments whose wines are trumpeted far and wide.

Why? This being primarily a tour guide, we were more impressed by people and places than ribbons and reviews. Sure, a particular small country winery might concoct a magnificent wine. But if it's produced and poured in an anonymous cinder-block warehouse, we'd rather order a case by mail and spend our Saturday visiting wineries with character and charm. Chances are good that we'll also discover a great new wine (or two) that the critics haven't heard of.

WINE RECOMMENDATIONS
While some wines improve with age, books that describe them don't. Because of their long shelf life, books simply are not very useful as consumer guides to specific vintages. (*Vintage* refers to the year during which the grapes were harvested and fermented.)

While visiting the small wineries featured in this guide, we discovered many wonderful vintages. Unfortunately, by the time the book went to press, most of the wares we sampled had been sold. (One winery we're familiar with produced only twenty-eight cases of a particular vintage.)

Consequently, enthusiastic endorsements and flowery descriptions of specific vintages aren't a part of this guide. We don't believe it serves any purpose to carry on about Ravenswood's 1989 Dickerson Vineyard Zinfandel when you can't buy a bottle. During the life of this book, the wineries included here will release other vintages that will surpass in quality some of the ones we tasted.

VINTNERS' CHOICES
Not wanting to send you blindly onto the back roads, we've asked the winemakers at each establishment to name a red and white of which they are consistently proud. While these "vintner's choice" wines might be subject to change from year to year, depending on the conditions, you'll have some idea about where a particular winery's strengths lie. Also included are observations about certain wines we enjoyed.

If you're interested in the current year's recommendations, pick up a copy of a wine or food magazine. Reviews of vintages from our backroad wineries are often included. In addition, many of the wineries described in these pages publish regular newsletters sharing information about new releases with customers. These are free and may be requested by phone, by writing, or at the time of your visit.

Better yet, jump in the car and make your own discoveries. If you wait to read about them in newspapers or magazines, you might be too late. On California's back roads, the early bird gets the best wine.

MAKING AN APPOINTMENT
Making an appointment to taste wine may sound somewhat off-putting, but owners of small wineries don't request it out of arrogance. These folks spend a good part of their day tending wines and vines. If you drop by unannounced, you may find your hosts in the lab, pruning vines, irrigating fields, or otherwise occupied. For most vintners who request a call in advance, twenty-four hours notice is generally sufficient.

RESPONSIBLE TOURING

Backroad wine touring can be one of the most pleasant ways to spend a day or a weekend. Don't spoil your day (or someone else's) by overindulging at the tasting bar or picnic table.

According to California Highway Patrol guidelines, drinking more than eight ounces of wine over a two-hour period could put you into the "driving under the influence" category. Remember, those wine samples add up quickly.

We suggest you designate a nondrinking driver for your winery tour and reward him or her with a bottle or two to enjoy later. Many wineries serve complimentary coffee, soda, or grape juice to designated drivers. Please do your part to keep the wine-country back roads safe.

A FOOTNOTE TO THE REVISED GUIDE

We didn't feel that our newly revised guide to small California wineries would be complete without some mention of two developments that are having a great impact on many of the state's vineyards during this decade.

PHYLLOXERA

No doubt by now most California wine enthusiasts have read about or witnessed the destructive effects on our vineyards of the phylloxera louse. This particularly virulent mutant strain of phylloxera, first spotted in Napa Valley in 1979, is now systematically working its way through the state. As this book went to press, more than fifteen thousand acres of vineyards in Napa and Sonoma counties had been infested. These prolific parasites can't be stopped by pesticides and ultimately kill the vines they attack.

Vineyard owners whose vines have become infested with phylloxeras have no choice but to replant with rootstock that is more resistant. You'll see many spindly young vines during your backroad winery tours as growers do battle with the destructive louse.

It's estimated that the infestation will cost grape growers and winemakers a half-billion dollars over the next decade or two. Expect at least part of the cost to be passed along to consumers in the form of higher wine prices, especially in the regions hardest hit by phylloxera.

ORGANIC FARMING

An increasing number of wines made by small Northern California wineries are being grown without the use of herbicides, chemical pesticides, or synthetic fertilizers. These carry labels bearing the term *organically grown*.

A federal law that took affect in October, 1993 requires that land be free from pesticides and other prohibited materials for three years prior to producing an organic crop.

Among the backroad winemakers embracing organic farming is Brian Fitzpatrick of Fitzpatrick Winery in Somerset. Brian is active with the California Certified Organic Farmers, an organization that sets organic standards and certifies that growers are in compliance.

Hallcrest Vineyards in the Santa Cruz mountains states that the organic process requires "much greater care in the entire process, since the wines are not protected by adding sulfites." (Many other organic wines still have added sulfites.)

Hallcrest's eight organic varietals are said to be among only a few nonsulfited wines available in the United States.

Though organic farming is catching on, fewer than five percent of California's acres planted to grapes crushed for wine and concentrate had been organically certified as we went to press with this edition.

BEFORE YOUR TOUR

Even though the winemaker or owner might be the one pouring samples at a backroad winery, don't be embarrassed if you're new to the winetasting game. Winemakers as well as tasting-bar hosts have their own special methods for tasting, and they're happy to pass along their techniques to visitors. You will generally start with dry white wines, moving next to sweet whites, and finishing with reds.

Lest they be intimidated by the process, visitors to Buena Vista Winery in Sonoma are greeted by printed instructions in the art of tasting. At Buena Vista, this is called the S method of tasting.

HOW TO TASTE WINE

SEE

Hold your glass at eye level and take note of the wine's color and clarity. The wine shouldn't appear cloudy or dull (sediment is okay). Red wines become lighter as they age, while white wines darken.

SWIRL

Gently swirl the glass, releasing the wine's aroma and bouquet. (*Aroma* is the smell of the grape in the wine; *bouquet* refers to the scents that result from aging and fermentation.)

SNIFF

Bring the glass close to your nose and inhale deeply. Try to pick out the different scents. Smelling a wine is important, since most of what you think is taste is in fact linked to smell. Most of the time you'll be greeted by pleasant aromas, but olfactory warning signs include a burning match smell (too much sulfur dioxide preservative) or a sour smell (too much acetic acid).

SIP

Take a sip of the wine and swirl it around in your mouth, making sure it encounters your whole tongue, so you'll be able to pick up all the subtle tastes. You'll notice definite flavors and sensations. Try to describe the wine's *body*, or mouthfeel. Is it light, medium, or full-bodied?

SAVOR

After you swallow, take a moment to savor the lingering tastes and sensations in your mouth. This impression is referred to as the wine's *finish*.

A FINAL NOTE

No payment was sought or accepted from any establishment in exchange for being featured in this book.

Bill Gleeson

Mendocino County

To Mendocino

To Eureka

1

128

Elk

Navarro

▼ **HANDLEY CELLARS**

HUSCH VINEYARDS ▼

▼ **LAZY CREEK VINEYARDS**

▼ **GREENWOOD RIDGE VINEYARDS**

101

▼ **NAVARRO VINEYARDS**

OBESTER WINERY ▼

Philo

Ukiah

Boonville

128

Cloverdale

Obester
TASTING ROOM

OBESTER WINERY

Philo

*O*bester Winery might be among the newer wineries along the Highway 128 wine road, but the owners, Paul and Sandy Obester, have roots planted deeply in the California wine industry.

Sandy's grandfather, the late John Gemello, figured prominently in the post-Repeal rebirth of the Santa Clara Valley wine industry with his own namesake winery. After retiring from Gemello Winery, the elder Gemello went to live with Sandy and Paul. In an attempt to provide her then-ninety-three-year-old grandfather with a project to occupy his time, Sandy suggested he teach the family how to make wine.

"It's strange the way things turn out," said Sandy, recalling the events that led her and Paul to establish their first winery near the Pacific Ocean in Half Moon Bay. "One thing led to another," she said, and the hobby evolved into a vocation when Paul, a Stanford University–educated Silicon Valley marketing executive, left his job to pursue a second career as winemaker. The Obesters bought land and established the Half Moon Bay operation in 1977.

The couple later expanded their vineyard holdings to include eighty acres in the Anderson Valley, and in 1989 they opened this second winery. About ten thousand cases of Anderson Valley wine are produced annually.

The centerpiece of the property is a handsome, Bungalow-style residence-turned-tasting room. Displayed on polished hardwood floors are several pieces of antiquated winemaking equipment that bring to mind the early days when John Gemello handcrafted his robust red wines.

Also sold in the tasting room is Gewurztraminer grape juice, organically grown apple juice, and a line of food products. Outside are rustic outbuildings, mature trees, and bountiful gardens, as well as gazebo-shaded picnic tables.

THE WINE LIST
Chardonnay
Sauvignon Blanc
Gewurztraminer
Johannisberg Riesling
Zinfandel
Pinot Noir
Sangiovese

VINTNER'S CHOICES
WHITE: *Sauvignon Blanc*
RED: *Zinfandel*

OBESTER WINERY
9200 HIGHWAY 128
PHILO, CA 95466
(707) 895-3814

HOURS: *10 a.m.–5 p.m. daily*
TASTINGS: *Yes*
CHARGE FOR TASTING: *No*
TOURS: *By appointment*
PICNIC AREA: *Yes*
RETAIL SALES: *Yes*

DIRECTIONS: *The winery is one-half mile south of Philo on Highway 128.*

NAVARRO VINEYARDS

Philo

"We looked for two years for someplace to grow Gewurztraminer," said Ted Bennett with a smile, as he recalled his decision in the mid-1970s to establish a winery specializing in the spicy Alsatian varietal. "The grape is hard to grow, the wine doesn't sell for a lot of money, and very few people can pronounce its name. You have to question our motivation."

One might also attribute such a brash move to unbridled ambition. After all, Ted had earlier founded the Pacific Stereo stores, built them into a successful chain, and sold out to CBS. Who wouldn't feel confident?

Someone else might have launched a new retail venture, but Ted` and his wife, Deborah Cahn, chose to invest their nest egg in the hills near tiny Philo in Mendocino County, where they set about planting Gewurztraminer vines in acres of limestone and clay.

While there may have been some scoffers in the beginning, no one questions Ted these days. He has again found himself at the helm of a successful venture, where demand for the product consistently outstrips supply. Navarro Vineyards has also earned more than one hundred awards, not only for the beloved Gewurztraminer but for other varietals, including Chardonnay and Pinot Noir.

THE WINE LIST
Gewurztraminer
Chardonnay
Sauvignon Blanc
Edelzwicker
Pinot Noir
Cabernet Sauvignon

VINTNER'S CHOICES
WHITE: *Gewurztraminer*
RED: *Pinot Noir*

NAVARRO VINEYARDS
5601 HIGHWAY 128
P.O. BOX #47
PHILO, CA 95466
(707) 895-3686;
TOLL-FREE (800) 537-9463

HOURS: *10 a.m.–5 p.m. daily*
TASTINGS: *Yes*
CHARGE FOR TASTING: *No*
TOURS: *By appointment*
PICNIC AREA: *Yes*
RETAIL SALES: *Yes*

DIRECTIONS: *Navarro Vineyards is located three miles north of Philo on Highway 128.*

Navarro wines are sampled in what we found to be the Philo area's most attractive and friendly tasting room. The handsome facility was crafted from three redwoods harvested from the nine-hundred-acre ranch. Arbor-covered tables are available for picnickers.

Most of the winery's staff, including Ted, pull tasting-bar duty, and all are well-informed about the products. Incidentally, most of Navarro's annual production of eighteen thousand cases is sold through the tasting room. It's a busy place.

At the time of our visit, Navarro was marketing a couple of noteworthy wines not generally available at our backroad destinations. Edelzwicker is a moderately priced, medal-winning, Alsatian-style blend of Gewurztraminer and Riesling. The winery's light and fruity Chardonnay table wine combines about 90 percent Chardonnay with small amounts of Sauvignon Blanc, Riesling, and (you guessed it) Gewurztraminer.

GREENWOOD RIDGE VINEYARDS

Philo

*D*on't let the small size of Greenwood Ridge Vineyards fool you. The little tasting room along Highway 128 might be easy to overlook, but its wines have made the big time.

Allan Green, a designer of magazines by original trade, has earned international acclaim for the wines produced by him and winemaker Van Williamson. Sweepstakes awards and gold medals for a varied product line that includes Merlot, Zinfandel, and Sauvignon Blanc have earned Greenwood Ridge a place of honor among our Northern California backroad wineries.

At the time of our visit, each of eight vintages had won multiple

prestigious awards. Greenwood Ridge's Chardonnay (1990), for example, won two gold, four silver, and two bronze awards from regional, state, and international competitions.

Greenwood Ridge's distinctive tasting room, set under a pyramid-shaped roof, is built into the side of a gentle hill. Pathways behind the building invite strolling. The actual winemaking facilities, which produce about five thousand cases per year, are seven miles away on Greenwood Road.

Allan's many interests are evidenced in the tasting room by a collection of more than two hundred wine cans, a sculpture made of five thousand wine corks, and a multisensory interpretation of

Greenwood Ridge wines — Allan's way of describing the essence of his wares. This "feast for the senses" (the packages are for sale) consists of three different wines, a musical cassette tape, and reproductions of paintings commissioned for and inspired by the wines.

For more than a decade, Greenwood Ridge has been the site of the annual California Wine Tasting Championships. Contestants — professional as well as novice and amateur — sample a series of wines and compete in identifying each by its varietal name. In the final round, extra points are given to those who can identify details such as appellation, vintage date, and producer.

The competition is held during the summer; entry forms are available by calling the winery.

THE WINE LIST
Sauvignon Blanc
Chardonnay
White Riesling
Late Harvest White Riesling
Cabernet Sauvignon
Pinot Noir
Zinfandel
Merlot

VINTNER'S CHOICES
WHITE: *White Riesling*
RED: *Cabernet Sauvignon*

GREENWOOD RIDGE VINEYARDS
5501 HIGHWAY 128
PHILO, CA 95466
(707) 895-2002

HOURS: *Summer: 10 a.m.– 6 p.m. daily; winter: 10 a.m.– 5 p.m. daily*
TASTINGS: *Yes*
CHARGE FOR TASTING: *No*
TOURS: *By appointment*
PICNIC AREA: *Yes*
RETAIL SALES: *Yes*

DIRECTIONS: *The Greenwood Ridge Vineyards tasting room is located three miles north of Philo on Highway 128.*

LAZY CREEK VINEYARDS

Philo

Unlike the Napa and Sonoma valleys, where remote back roads lead to tiny hidden wineries, Mendocino County offers few such hidden gems. You won't need a map to visit this region's wineries, most of which sit right alongside Highway 128.

However, by asking around a bit, we were able to find one small, off-the-beaten-track winemaking operation that proved to be a pleasant surprise.

From Highway 128, we turned onto a dirt road (only a mail box address marks the spot) that meanders along a lane flanked by moss-laden split-rail fences and a dense growth of trees. The road crosses

Lazy Creek three times before dead-ending at the home and winery of Hans and Theresia Kobler.

Hans and Theresia didn't intend to become winemakers when they left their native Switzerland in 1960. Trained in the restaurant industry, Hans served as a captain at the famous Brown Derby in Hollywood.

Although the original plan was to take what Hans learned about American restaurants back home, the Koblers ultimately decided not to return to Switzerland, opting instead to grow grapes in Mendocino County. They started making wine as a way to supplement the family income when the price of grapes took a tumble.

Although annual production has never been more than five thousand cases, Lazy Creek has become well known, especially among Gewurztraminer connoisseurs. Some critics have called the Kobler family's Gewurztraminer the best in the state.

The small, rustic winery, reportedly the oldest in Anderson Valley, sits behind the family's home along Lazy Creek. Three small buildings comprise the operation, whose remote location allowed it to turn out wine during Prohibition. Tastings are often conducted outdoors under the branches of a huge walnut tree.

THE WINE LIST
Gewurztraminer
Chardonnay
Pinot Noir

VINTNER'S CHOICES
WHITE: *Gewurztraminer*
RED: *Pinot Noir*

LAZY CREEK VINEYARDS
4610 HIGHWAY 128
PHILO, CA 95466
(707) 895-3623

HOURS: *Daily, by appointment only*
TASTINGS: *By appointment*
CHARGE FOR TASTING: *No*
TOURS: *Informal*
PICNIC AREA: *Yes*
RETAIL SALES: *Yes*

DIRECTIONS: *The winery's driveway, between Greenwood Ridge Winery and Roederer Estate, is unmarked, except for a mailbox located on the east side of the highway with the numbers 4610. At the mailbox, follow the dirt drive east to the Koblers' house. The winery is located behind the home.*

HUSCH VINEYARDS

Philo

It's true that a few grape growers cultivated the Anderson Valley soil many generations ago, but it wasn't until Tony and Gretchen Husch bonded their namesake winery in 1971 that wine aficionados took serious notice.

Also taking note were Hugo Oswald and his grape-growing family, who ended up buying the winery in 1979. The three generations of winemaking Oswalds combined the sixty-some-acre Husch and nearby Day Ranch properties with their La Ribera Vineyard along the Russian

River in nearby Ukiah Valley.

Although a couple of decades have brought many new wineries to the valley — there are competitors to the north, south, and east — Husch is still a highly respected name in the Northern California wine industry.

It's also a delightful place to visit. After a stop at the little old granary-turned-tasting room, we strolled up the dirt drive past a couple of picnic tables and through the vines to an old barn at the highest part of the property. The panorama takes in much of the Husch holdings, as well as the Roederer Estate winery just across the road.

At the time of our visit, Husch was tempting travelers with a Reserve Chardonnay and a very tasty, moderately priced white table wine (a Sauvignon Blanc and Chardonnay blend), both of which are sold only at the tasting room and a few local outlets.

When grape-growing conditions are favorable, the winery produces a Cabernet table wine that can be enjoyed immediately. Each year Husch also creates a nonalcoholic juice made from estate varietals. This is another product available only locally.

THE WINE LIST
Cabernet Sauvignon
Pinot Noir
La Ribera Cabernet table wine
La Ribera Blanc table wine
Chardonnay
Chenin Blanc
Gewurztraminer
Sauvignon Blanc
Nonalcoholic grape juice

VINTNER'S CHOICES
WHITE: *Chardonnay*
RED: *Pinot Noir*

HUSCH VINEYARDS
4400 HIGHWAY 128
PHILO, CA 95466
(707) 895-3216

HOURS: *Summer: 10 a.m.–6 p.m. daily; Winter: 10 a.m.–5 p.m. daily*
TASTINGS: *Yes*
CHARGE FOR TASTING: *No*
TOURS: *By appointment*
PICNIC AREA: *Yes*
RETAIL SALES: *Yes*

DIRECTIONS: *The winery is five miles west of Philo on Highway 128.*

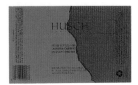

HANDLEY CELLARS

Philo

Something in the genes probably led winemaker Milla Handley to study enology and spend hours in the basement of her home handcrafting small batches of Chardonnay. After all, her great-great-grandfather, brewer Henry Weinhard, knew a thing or two about fermentation science (although Henry used hops and barley instead of grapes).

After earning her degree at the University of California, Davis, Milla practiced her craft for five years at Château St. Jean and at Edmeades Winery before establishing Handley Cellars in her home basement, with husband Rex McClellan. Their first release, a 1982 Chardonnay, grabbed a gold medal at the Orange County Fair's prestigious wine competition.

After outgrowing their cramped subterranean digs, Milla and Rex built a more functional winery nearby. The sunny tasting room doubles

as a museum, containing dozens of pieces from the Handley family's international collection. These include an elephant-shaped table and chairs, Asian statues, Mexican masks, and Indonesian carvings. Outside in the garden patio area, a statue of Buddha sits before the fermentation tanks.

Handley Cellars' product line includes a blend of White Riesling and Gewurztraminer called Brightlighter White, as well as three sparkling wines — all varying blends of Chardonnay and Pinot Noir.

THE WINE LIST
Chardonnay
Sauvignon Blanc
Brightlighter White
Gewurztraminer
Pinot Noir
Brut sparkling wine
Brut Rosé sparkling wine
Blanc de Blancs sparkling wine

VINTNER'S CHOICES
WHITE: *Chardonnay*
RED: *Brut Rosé sparkling wine*

HANDLEY CELLARS
3151 HIGHWAY 128
PHILO, CA 95466
(707) 895-2190

HOURS: *Summer: 11 a.m.–6 p.m. daily; Winter: 11 a.m.–5 p.m. daily*
TASTINGS: *Yes*
CHARGE FOR TASTING: *No*
TOURS: *By appointment*
PICNIC AREA: *Yes*
RETAIL SALES: *Yes*

DIRECTIONS: *Six miles west of Philo on Highway 128.*

Sonoma County

Alexander
Valley Rd.

▼ SAUSAL WINERY

MILL CREEK VINEYARDS ▼

▼ JORDAN
VINEYARDS

▼ JOHNSON'S ALEXANDER
VALLEY WINES

Westside   Road

▼ ALEXANDER VALLEY
VINEYARDS

Healdsburg

▼ HOP KILN
WINERY

▼ FIELD STONE WINERY

Chalk   Hill Rd.

TOPOLOS AT ▼
RUSSIAN RIVER
VINEYARDS

IRON HORSE ▼
VINEYARDS

Sebastopol

101

116

Santa Rosa

▼ ADLER FELS WINERY

▼ RAVENSWOOD WINERY

12

▼ BUENA VISTA WINERY

▼ GUNDLACH-BUNDSCHU
WINERY

Sonoma

101

121

BUENA VISTA WINERY

Sonoma

Buena Vista isn't quite typical of Northern California's small mom-and-pop wineries. It's a major producer (a quarter of a million cases per year) and is owned by a foreign corporation. Still, we believe backroad winery travelers, especially first-time visitors, will enjoy a visit to what is generally considered to be the birthplace of California's premium wine industry.

If Buena Vista is the oldest premium winery in the state, Agoston Haraszthy, the Hungarian aristocrat–turned–California vintner, must be the industry's patriarch. A one-time bodyguard of Emperor Ferdinand of Austria-Hungary, Haraszthy fled his homeland after being marked for death following a revolution in the 1840s. He ended up in the United States and traveled from east to west scouting a vineyard site. After sampling wines from the Sonoma estate of General Mariano Vallejo, Haraszthy knew he'd found the spot, and in 1857 began construction of the winery and a grand Italian-style villa. (The mansion burned a few years later.)

In 1861 Haraszthy convinced California officials to send him to Europe, where he collected *vinifera* vines. The Count, as he was known, returned with some one hundred thousand cuttings,

Continued next page

THE WINE LIST
Chardonnay
Sauvignon Blanc
Johannisberg Riesling
Gewurztraminer
Cabernet Sauvignon
Pinot Noir
Merlot
Gamay Beaujolais

VINTNER'S CHOICES
WHITE: *Chardonnay*
RED: *Cabernet Sauvignon*

BUENA VISTA WINERY
18000 OLD WINERY ROAD
SONOMA, CA 95476
(800) 926-1266

HOURS: *10 a.m.–5 p.m. daily*
TASTINGS: *Yes*
CHARGE FOR TASTING:
Downstairs, no; upstairs, yes
TOURS: *Yes*
PICNIC AREA: *Yes*
RETAIL SALES: *Yes*

DIRECTIONS: *From Highway 12 just off Sonoma Plaza, drive east on East Napa Street, and turn left on Old Winery Road. Follow to winery parking area.*

which were distributed to growers throughout the region. Haraszthy's own vineyards became one of the largest wine estates in the world.

Unfortunately, the winery was soon dealt a triple whammy. On an 1869 trip to Central America, Haraszthy disappeared (evidence pointed to a particularly large crocodile); phylloxera lice devastated the vineyards; and the 1906 San Francisco earthquake collapsed the wine tunnels.

The property languished for decades, until war correspondent Frank Bartholomew stepped in and replanted vines and restored the historic buildings. The current owner, German-based A. Racke Company, bought Buena Vista in 1979.

To reach the spacious estate, closed to auto traffic, you'll walk along a pedestrian road flanked by blackberry bushes and towering eucalyptus trees. The first stop is the original press house, built in 1863. The two-level stone building today serves as tasting room, gift shop, and gallery. Current Buena Vista wines are poured at the downstairs bar (no charge), while older vintages can be tasted upstairs (for a fee) at the Heritage Tasting Room.

Unfortunately, time and earthquakes have weakened the walls and ceiling of the old cellar, which is now gated and closed to visitors, pending major structural work. However, the historical information and relics that once were on display in the cellar have been moved outside, and guided tours of the property are offered daily at 2 p.m. Don't expect to watch winemaking in action here. Buena Vista grapes are grown on a large vineyard in the Carneros region, where the winery and winemaking activities are also located.

GUNDLACH-BUNDSCHU WINERY

Sonoma

If walls could talk, this winery could tell many tales about the trials and tribulations of one of California's oldest winemaking families.

Jacob Gundlach's persistent struggle to start a new life as a California winemaker was marked both by hardship and good fortune. First there was the storm that wrecked his ship on the trip around Cape Horn from Europe. He spent more than a month as an island castaway before reaching San Francisco in 1851.

Next came the backbreaking cultivation of his four-hundred-acre Rhinefarm in Sonoma Valley with a horse-drawn, single-blade plow, and the arduous process of hand-picking grapes and hauling sixty-pound lugs.

In 1874 the destructive phylloxera louse worked its way through California's vineyards and into Gundlach's prized vines. Fortunately,

Rhinefarm's vineyard master discovered that native American vines resisted the disease, and work began to graft the domestic rootstock

Continued next page

THE WINE LIST

Kleinberger, a little-known German varietal
Sonoma White table wine
Gewurztraminer
Riesling
Chardonnay
Sonoma Red table wine
Zinfandel
Cabernet Franc
Cabernet Sauvignon
Merlot
Gamay Beaujolais
Pinot Noir

VINTNER'S CHOICES
WHITE: *Gewurztraminer*
RED: *Merlot*

GUNDLACH BUNDSCHU WINERY
2000 DENMARK STREET
SONOMA, CA 95476
(707) 938-5277

HOURS: *11 a.m.–4:30 p.m. daily*
TASTINGS: *Yes*
CHARGE FOR TASTING: *No*
TOURS: *Self-guided*
PICNIC AREA: *Yes*
RETAIL SALES: *Yes*

DIRECTIONS: *From Sonoma Plaza, drive east on Napa Street, right on Eighth Street East, and left on Denmark Street. Watch for the winery sign on the left.*

onto the existing vines. (Incidentally, it was Jacob who introduced California to the now-famous German varietal we call Johannisberg, or White, Riesling.)

Things went well over the next few years as Jacob and his partner and son-in-law, Charles Bundschu, built a thriving business, winning a loyal following on both coasts.

Tragedy struck again in 1906, when Jacob watched the great earthquake and fire reduce the partners' massive San Francisco warehouse to rubble. Rhinefarm was untouched, and the business continued.

The next blow was dealt not by nature but by the government. Although the vineyards continued to be cultivated during the thirteen years of Prohibition, the winery closed its doors, and Gundlach-

Bundschu was disbanded. A fire later gutted the abandoned winery.

The family held onto the property, and Walter Bundschu, Jacob's great-grandson, began growing grapes some years later. He was succeeded by his son, Towle Bundschu.

Towle's son, Jim, revitalized the company in the late 1960s by rebuilding the winery and restarting the crusher, resuming one of California's oldest and proudest winemaking businesses.

Although first-time visitors might have a bit of trouble finding Gundlach-Bundschu, this is our favorite Sonoma Valley winery and is well worth the search. The tasting room is friendly (your tasting will likely be accompanied by vintage rock music) and there's much to see outside. Don't leave without enjoying the outdoor art or taking the short trail to an oak- and eucalyptus-studded hilltop picnic area. It's one of Sonoma's choicest spots.

Finally, some of Gundlach-Bundschu wines are stoppered with corks imprinted with fortunes. No, the author isn't Confucius; it's Bacchus. A sample: "Leave the land and money to the kids; drink the wine yourself."

RAVENSWOOD

Sonoma

If you ventured out Gehricke Road during the 1980s to visit Peter Haywood's winery, it's time to make another pilgrimage. The operation changed hands (and winemakers) in 1991 and is known now as Ravenswood.

Immunologist-turned-winemaker Joel Peterson has increased production to about forty thousand cases per year, much of it Zinfandel. One of the country's best-known producers of Zin, Joel is so passionate about this robust wine that he was making five types during our last visit. All but one were vineyard-specific. The other, a Zinfandel vintners blend, was intended to be enjoyed young.

In addition to Cabernet Sauvignon, Merlot, and a few hundred cases of Chardonnay, Ravenswood produces Vin Gris, a rose-colored wine made by removing some of the juice from Cabernet Sauvignon and  Cabernet Franc grapes after crushing but before much color is extracted from the skins.

The winery, which sits above the road and looks out over acres of vineyards, is a modest-looking operation with a small-but-friendly tasting room. On chilly days it's warmed by a woodburning stove. A couple of tables are placed on the patio out front.

The circle of three ravens that comprises the distinctive label was designed by poster artist David Lance Goines.

THE WINE LIST
Chardonnay
Vin Gris
Merlot
Zinfandel
Cabernet Sauvignon

VINTNER'S CHOICES
WHITE: *Sangiacomo Vineyard Chardonnay*
RED: *Dickerson Vineyard Zinfandel*

RAVENSWOOD
18701 GEHRICKE ROAD
SONOMA, CA 95476
(707) 938-1960

HOURS: *10 a.m.– 4:30 p.m. daily*
TASTINGS: *Yes*
CHARGE FOR TASTING: *No*
TOURS: *Yes*
PICNIC AREA: *Yes*
RETAIL SALES: *Yes*

DIRECTIONS: *From Sonoma Plaza, drive east on Napa Street and turn left on Fourth Street East. Turn right on Lovall Valley Road and left on Gehricke to winery on left.*

ADLER FELS WINERY

Santa Rosa

though the golf tee on the cliff (clubs and balls provided) might seem a bit unusual to the first-time visitor, you'll come to appreciate it after getting to know Adler Fels' "individualistic, stylized wines" and its equally individualistic vintner David Coleman.

David and his wife, Ayn (pronounced Ann) Ryan, have been tweaking the traditions of California's wine industry ever since they built their hilltop winery in 1979.

As Adler Fels' winemaker and guiding spirit, David has earned a reputation as being delightfully outspoken. And while his wines have been described in such varied terms as "lush," "quirky," "beautiful," and "strangest of strange," they're rarely maligned. Quite the contrary. At the time of our visit, Adler Fels' Fume Blanc had been winning one or more gold medals for eight consecutive vintages. Although wine writer Jerry Mead once described David's Mélange a Deux (a sparkling wine) as "too weird" to score, he concluded by saying, "I do like it."

Over the years, Adler Fels has evolved into a white wine specialist,

with David buying grapes selectively from Sonoma County growers. They own no vineyards, since David believes good grapes grow in the particular microregions to which they are best suited. "It's impossible to plant thirty- or forty-year-old vines," noted David. "But I can certainly buy grapes from them."

With no vineyards to care for, David has more time to conjure up ways to make better wine. Formerly an industrial designer, he invented the variable capacity fermenting tank whose floating lid rests on the wine. In addition to eliminating the use of nitrogen, which robs the wine of color, smell, and flavor, the tight-fitting lid reduces the use of sulphur (since the threat of oxidation is lessened). The result-ing wines have a more intense varietal character and boast some of the lowest sulfite levels in the industry. (Other wines have as much as four times the sulfite levels of Adler Fels'.)

David also built the winery — by hand. Set against a breathtak-ing backdrop of hills and big sky, the structure's towers and half-timbered façade give it a decidedly fairy-tale appearance.

No stranger to the winery business herself, Ayn is from a Porterville, California, winemaking family and has been in charge of marketing Adler Fels wines since 1980.

Oh, about that golf tee. Guests who make an appointment to visit are encouraged to drive a ball or two off a rugged, fifteen-hundred-foot cliff into the wilds beyond. As Ayn says, "It's a great way to get a little exercise or entertain someone who'd rather play golf than talk wine." You'll even be presented with a custom score card suitable for framing. And you won't be asked to retrieve the ball.

THE WINE LIST
Fume Blanc
Chardonnay (two types)
Gewurztraminer
Mélange a Deux, a proprietary
    sparkling wine

VINTNER'S CHOICES
WHITE: *Fume Blanc and*
    Gewurztraminer

ADLER FELS WINERY
5325 CORRICK LANE
SANTA ROSA, CA 95409
(707) 539-3123

HOURS: *By appointment only*
TASTINGS: *By appointment*
CHARGE FOR TASTING: *No*
TOURS: *By appointment*
PICNIC AREA: *No (although sometimes available for small groups)*
RETAIL SALES: *By appointment*

DIRECTIONS: *From Highway 12 east of Santa Rosa, drive north on Los Alamos Road for 2.2 miles. Turn left at Corrick Lane and winery gate and drive one-quarter mile to winery on left.*

IRON HORSE VINEYARDS

Sebastopol

It was during his thirtieth birthday trip to France that bicoastal attorney Barry Sterling vowed to one day live there. A high achiever known for taking charge of his own destiny, Barry joined an international law firm a few years later and, sure enough, went to work in the Paris office.

Avid travelers, Barry and his wife, Audrey, toured Europe extensively, searching out fine restaurants, galleries, antique shops, and wineries. The couple's appreciation of wine flourished, and they ultimately collected more than four thousand bottles of Europe's finest vintages.

In 1967 the Sterlings began a nearly decade-long international search for a wine estate. The quest ended in the hills near Sebastopol, where they stumbled on Iron Horse Ranch. The ranch's vineyards had only partially been developed, and the nineteenth-century carpenter Gothic house was in dire straits.

Over the next several years, Barry and Audrey, along with partner and winemaker Forrest Tancer, restored the vines, constructed the winery buildings, renovated the house, and began making wines. The first were made in 1979.

One year later, the winery found its niche when a decision was made to craft a small amount of sparkling wine. These days, Iron Horse sparklers, which account for about 50 percent of its annual production, are widely and consistently acclaimed. They're often compared favorably to the Champagnes of France.

Iron Horse was the official toasting wine at Mikhail Gorbachev's historic meetings with Presidents George Bush and Ronald Reagan and more recently was chosen as the celebration wine for the Clintons and Gores on election night in 1992.

Iron Horse wines are created in a big red barnlike building that rises from the estate's hillside vineyards. When the weather is cooperative, tastings are conducted just outside the winery, where a million-dollar view unfolds.

For those not acquainted with sparkling wines, it might be useful to know that those labeled Blanc de Blancs are made from Chardonnay grapes. For Blanc de Noirs, winemakers use Pinot Noir, Gamay, and Cabernet Sauvignon. Brut is the driest sparkling wine.

THE WINE LIST
Vintage Brut
Vintage Blanc de Noirs
Vintage Blanc de Blancs
Vintage Brut Rosé
Vintage Late Disgorged Brut
Chardonnay
Fume Blanc
*Cabernets, a proprietary blend of
    Cabernet Sauvignon and
    Cabernet Franc*
Pinot Noir

VINTNER'S CHOICES
WHITE: *Blanc de Blancs*
RED: *Blanc de Noirs*

**IRON HORSE VINEYARDS
9786 ROSS STATION ROAD
SEBASTOPOL, CA 95472
(707) 887-1507**

HOURS: *By appointment*
TASTINGS: *By appointment*
CHARGE FOR TASTING: *No*
TOURS: *By appointment*
PICNIC AREA: *No*
RETAIL SALES: *Yes*

DIRECTIONS: *At the intersection of Highway 116 and Ross Station Road south of Forestville (on downhill side of Kozlowski Farms), drive west on Ross Station Road to winery.*

TOPOLOS AT RUSSIAN RIVER VINEYARDS

Forestville

long Sonoma County's scenic Gravenstein Highway, the Topolos family's towered redwood winery attracts more than its fair share of stares. In designing a building in which to make north coast wines, the winery's architects borrowed from a classic regional architectural theme: the hop kilns of the Sonoma Valley and Fort Ross, the historic Russian settlement on the Mendocino Coast.

Founded in 1963 as Russian River Vineyards, the winery was purchased in 1978 by Michael Topolos and his Bay Area businessman

brother, Jerry. In assuming duties as vintner, Michael drew on his experience as a merchant du vin for a San Francisco grocer and his studies at the University of California, Davis.

Although Topolos at Russian River Vineyards makes a few white wines, it's known primarily for reds. In crafting three different Zinfandels, Michael had in mind the legions of White Zinfandel lovers who resist moving on to the bolder red cousin. He has created what he calls a three-tiered program that can lure the White Zinfandel drinker into bigger and better Zinfandels.

Topolos Sonoma Zinfandel (the winery's least expensive) is a light-bodied, light-hearted wine that should be most appealing to White Zin lovers. It's made with a small amount of white grapes. The Zinfandel from old Rossi Ranch vines is a bigger, more powerful wine, while the Zinfandel Ultimo was described by one wine writer as possibly "too big." It's a wine that should benefit from aging.

The dramatic winery is only part of the family's complex. The Topoloses operate a highly rated restaurant in an adjacent century-old home (Jerry and wife Christine oversee this part of the business) and a tasting room that has recently been brightened up and redecorated with handsome custom woodwork and pavers.

At this writing, Michael was only one of a couple of California vintners making Alicante Bouschet, a deep-colored red wine from a French hybrid grape whose juice is nearly black. Production of this special collectors' wine is limited.

THE WINE LIST
Sauvignon Blanc
Chardonnay
Gewurztraminer
Alicante Fresco
Cabernet Blanc
Brut
Pinot Noir
Zinfandel
Cabernet Sauvignon
Petite Sirah
Grand Noir, a Rhône-style red
Alicante Bouschet

VINTNER'S CHOICES
WHITE: *Chardonnay*
RED: *Zinfandel, Rossi Ranch*

TOPOLOS AT RUSSIAN RIVER VINEYARDS
5700 GRAVENSTEIN HIGHWAY NORTH
FORESTVILLE, CA 95436
(707) 887-1575

HOURS: *10:30 a.m.–5:30 p.m. daily*
TASTINGS: *Yes*
CHARGE FOR TASTING: *No*
TOURS: *By appointment*
PICNIC AREA: *No*
RETAIL SALES: *Yes*

DIRECTIONS: *From Highway 101 near Santa Rosa, drive west on Highway 12 to Sebastopol, then north on Highway 116 (Gravenstein Highway) for five miles to winery on left.*

HOP KILN WINERY

Healdsburg

When Dr. Martin Griffin purchased a 240-acre Sonoma County sheep ranch with an eye toward retirement, a derelict, triple-towered hop kiln and cooling/baling barn came as part of the deal. After one of the kiln's towers toppled in a windstorm, and as the two sections of barn grew weaker, Martin, a doctor of internal medicine-turned-public health officer, intervened.

In order to finance an extensive effort to restore the turn-of-the-century kiln, Martin decided to create a winery on the property.

It wasn't a spur-of-the-moment decision, however. Martin had earlier studied winemaking in Italy, and his Healdsburg property included an old vineyard of Zinfandel and Petite Sirah. Grapes from these vines were used to make wine for workers during the thirty-five-or-so years that the structure served as a kiln. Martin increased the acreage, and in 1974 the completely restored Hop Kiln Winery crushed its first grapes.

Now retired from medicine and less active in the winery's day-to-day operations, Martin resides in a stately Italianate Victorian manse that was moved in pieces from nearby Fulton and reassembled near the winery.

Visitors are received in the rustic barn connected to the kiln. An art gallery displaying works of local artists occupies one wall. Part of a rear-facing wall has given way to a large window that affords views of the vineyards and an adjacent pond. Picnic tables are set up near the water's edge.

Winery equipment is located outside the structure, while wines age in barrels stored in a dark, cool environment behind the kiln's stone walls. About nine thousand cases are produced annually.

THE WINE LIST
Chardonnay
Gewurztraminer
Johannisberg Riesling
*Sparkling Johannisberg
   Riesling*
*Valdiguie (formerly Napa
   Gamay)*
Zinfandel
Petite Sirah
Cabernet Sauvignon
*Marty Griffin's Big Red, a
   full-bodied blend of Gamay,
   Zinfandel, and Cabernet
   Sauvignon*
*A Thousand Flowers, a
   blended white table wine*

VINTNER'S CHOICES
WHITE: *Chardonnay*
RED: *Zinfandel*

**HOP KILN WINERY
6050 WESTSIDE ROAD
HEALDSBURG, CA 95448
(707) 433-6491**

HOURS: *10 a.m.–5 p.m. daily*
TASTINGS: *Yes*
CHARGE FOR TASTING: *No*
TOURS: *No*
PICNIC AREA: *Yes*
RETAIL SALES: *Yes*

DIRECTIONS: *From Highway 101 north, take the second Healdsburg exit and make an immediate left onto Mill Street (this becomes Westside Road). Follow Westside Road for approximately six miles to winery on left.*

MILL CREEK VINEYARDS

Healdsburg

*H*op Kiln Winery isn't Dry Creek Valley's only improbable winemaking facility. If Martin Griffin can operate a successful winery out of an old hop kiln, why not market wines from a working replica of a New England mill?

The Kreck family, former cattle ranchers who moved from Southern California to Sonoma County in the late 1940s, constructed the pic-

turesque little mill in 1982 to show-case their wines. And they haven't been disappointed. Outside, the turning water wheel lures a steady stream of Westside Road motorists who stop, snap a picture or two, and taste some of the Kreck's wines.

Two generations work the business these days. Chuck (the father) is the proprietor, Vera (the mother) manages the tasting room, and sons Bill and Robert serve as general manager and vineyard manager respectively.

Although the mill has become a backroad winery landmark of sorts, the remote picnic area at the rear of the property is still somewhat of a secret. A short but steep hike up the hill behind the mill will bring you to a spacious deck whose picnic tables command an unsurpassed view of the valley.

THE WINE LIST
Chardonnay
Sauvignon Blanc
Gewurztraminer
Old Mill White table wine
Cabernet Blush
Merlot
Cabernet Sauvignon
Old Mill Red table wine

VINTNER'S CHOICES
WHITE: *Gewurztraminer*
RED: *Merlot*

MILL CREEK VINEYARDS
1401 WESTSIDE ROAD
HEALDSBURG, CA 95448
(707) 433-5098

HOURS: *12 p.m.–5 p.m. Monday through Friday; 11 a.m.–5 p.m. weekends. Winery is closed Tuesday through Thursday from November through March.*
TASTINGS: *Yes*
CHARGE FOR TASTING: *No*
TOURS: *No*
PICNIC AREA: *Yes*
RETAIL SALES: *Yes*

DIRECTIONS: *From Highway 101 north, take the second Healdsburg exit and make an immediate left onto Mill Street (this becomes Westside Road). Follow Westside Road to winery on right.*

JORDAN VINEYARD AND WINERY

Healdsburg

If pressed to name one back-country California winery as an absolute must-see, the sprawling Bordeaux-style Jordan château comes immediately to mind. However, we were sworn to secrecy about its exact location off Alexander Valley Road. The Jordan people prefer to give directions when you call for an appointment.

The first hint of something special is the long, twisting lane that winds past moss-laden oaks over gentle hills. At the end of the road, the mustard-colored winery unfolds in a magnificent scene right out of a French postcard. There simply is no other winery like it in California.

The baronial estate was created by Tom and Sally Jordan in the early 1970s, fulfilling the owners' longtime dream. Tom, formerly a geologist lawyer and Colorado state legislator, earned his fortune in oil exploration and sank millions of dollars into these gorgeous Sonoma County foothills, striving to create wines that would compete with the best from France.

In the process he carved out hundreds of acres of new vineyards — 275 acres to date — and erected what the *New York Times* called "one of the most spectacular wineries in North America."

Visitors who take the public tour will catch some tempting glimpses of the grand Jordan style. You'll be able to peek into the grand formal dining room, site of lavish feasts for those who market Jordan wines, and stroll through the pristine winemaking facilities, including a barrel room lit by chandeliers and framed by Douglas fir beams.

In keeping with the formal Jordan atmosphere, there's no winery gift shop offering T-shirts or personalized corkscrews. There's not even a public tasting room. Wines are discreetly sold out of a large armoire.

THE WINE LIST
Chardonnay
Cabernet Sauvignon

VINTNER'S CHOICES
WHITE: *Estate Bottled*
     Chardonnay
RED: *Estate Bottled Cabernet*
     Sauvignon

JORDAN VINEYARD AND WINERY
P.O. BOX 878
HEALDSBURG, CA 95448
(707) 431-5250

HOURS: *By appointment*
TASTINGS: *No*
TOURS: *By appointment*
PICNIC AREA: *No*
RETAIL SALES: *Yes*

DIRECTIONS: *Map furnished with letter confirming tour appointment.*

SAUSAL WINERY

Healdsburg

When you visit Sausal Winery, chances are you'll meet at least one staffer named Demostene. From the outside (where brothers David and Ed handle winemaking and vineyard care) to the inside (where sisters Roselee and Cindy run the tasting room and office), this operation is all in the family.

The Demostene siblings are carrying forth a tradition that started with Abel Ferrari, who left Italy for Northern California just after the turn of the century. A machinist who invented grape-crushing and juice-pumping

equipment still used today, Abel ultimately opened his own machine shop in downtown Healdsburg — the business is still there — and bought into Soda Rock Winery as a partner.

Abel's son-in-law, Leo Demostene, became the winemaker at Soda Rock and later introduced his own sons, David and Ed, to the trade as young children.

Leo and his wife, Rose, purchased the Sausal Ranch in 1956 with the intention of converting 125 acres of prunes and apples (and some grapes) into vineyards and starting a new winery. Although Leo died before his dream could be realized, the children forged ahead and turned an old prune dehydrator into a winery. Their first crush was in 1973.

It wasn't until the mid-1980s that the tasting room was built, giving the winery wider exposure. The resulting additional business also nearly doubled Sausal's annual production, which now stands at around fifteen thousand cases.

Although known primarily for its Zinfandel, one of the winery's most popular products is Sausal Blanc, a blend of French Colombard, Chardonnay, and Chenin Blanc.

THE WINE LIST
Chardonnay
Sausal Blanc
White Zinfandel
Zinfandel
Cabernet Sauvignon

VINTNER'S CHOICES
WHITE: *Sausal Blanc*
RED: *Zinfandel*

SAUSAL WINERY
7370 HIGHWAY 128
HEALDSBURG, CA 95448
(707) 433-2285

HOURS: *10 a.m.– 4 p.m. daily*
TASTINGS: *Yes*
CHARGE FOR TASTING: *No*
TOURS: *No*
PICNIC AREA: *Yes*
RETAIL SALES: *Yes*

DIRECTIONS: *From Highway 101, drive east on Dry Creek Road. Turn left on Healdsburg Avenue and right on Alexander Valley Road (becomes Highway 128) to winery on left, just after the sharp right turn.*

JOHNSON'S ALEXANDER VALLEY WINES

Healdsburg

For many backroad wine-country travelers, meeting folks like Tom and Gail Johnson is what makes a visit to a small family-owned winery a memorable experience. This happy clan isn't driven to set the wine world afire. For Tom, Gail, and their daughter, starting a small winery was a labor of love. But the business was a long time coming.

The land under Johnson's Alexander Valley Wines wasn't always a vineyard. The family farm began as a fruit ranch back in 1952, under

the direction of Tom's father, producing pears, prunes, and some grapes.

A plot of premium vines was started in the mid-1960s, and a few years later Tom and Gail took over the ranch. The barn, built in the 1880s, was refurbished, and by 1975 the Johnsons had themselves a full-fledged winery.

Tom heads the operation; Gail can often be found in the tasting room; and their daughter, Ellen, a California State University, Fresno, alumnus, fills the role of winemaker.

The Johnsons prefer to keep production comparatively low — only four thousand cases per year — and the tasting room rustic and informal. Visitors to the Johnson property have been known to do a double take upon approaching the winery, from which the sounds of a vintage theater pipe organ can often be heard. The Johnsons crank up the contraption during harvest season, at the winery's annual anniversary party, for Tom's birthday, or whenever the mood (or the wine) inspires them.

THE WINE LIST
Chardonnay
Johannisberg Riesling
Pinot Noir
Zinfandel
Cabernet Sauvignon

VINTNER'S CHOICES
WHITE: *Chardonnay*
RED: *Pinot Noir*

JOHNSON'S ALEXANDER VALLEY WINES
8333 HIGHWAY 128
HEALDSBURG, CA 95448
(707) 433-2319

HOURS: *10 a.m.–5 p.m. daily*
TASTINGS: *Yes*
CHARGE FOR TASTING: *No*
TOURS: *On request or appointment*
PICNIC AREA: *Yes*
RETAIL SALES: *Yes*

DIRECTIONS: *From Highway 101, drive east on Dry Creek Road. Turn left on Healdsburg Avenue and right on Alexander Valley Road (becomes Highway 128) to winery on right, one and one-half miles after the sharp right turn.*

ALEXANDER VALLEY VINEYARDS

Healdsburg

Wine grapes represent only one of the myriad crops that have flourished on the estate now known as Alexander Valley Vineyards. In the 1840s, Cyrus Alexander directed the establishment of a vast agricultural tract that included fruit trees, vegetable gardens, wheat fields, hops, and cattle and sheep ranches.

Recruited by landowner Henry Fitch to open the virgin northern section of his three-hundred-thousand-acre Sotoyome Grant, Alexander became the first European settler of the valley that now

bears his name. He over-
saw the ranch for a share
of land and ultimately
was given title to some
nine thousand acres.

The property remained
in the Alexander family
until 1963, when Los
Angeles manufacturing
company executive
Harry Wetzel, Jr., purchased several hundred acres, including the old
Alexander home, for use as a vacation residence. At about the time the
family began replanting some of the aging vineyards, son Harry III
(Hank) developed a keen interest in winemaking. He enrolled at the
University of California, Davis, and graduated in 1973. Construction of
the winery began that year.

Hank and sister Katie Wetzel Murphy run the business today from
the early California–style winery situated on a hillside a stone's throw
from the restored Alexander homestead. A dark-stained board-and-
batten tasting room sits atop the cellar. The winery, tucked amid vines
and moss-laden oak at the edge of the valley, produces about forty-five
thousand cases per year.

Visitors may sample Alexander Valley Vineyards' estate-bottled
wines in the antique-furnished tasting room or soak up countryside
views from the veranda.

THE WINE LIST
Chardonnay
Dry Chenin Blanc
Johannisberg Riesling
Gewurztraminer
Cabernet Sauvignon
Pinot Noir
Zinfandel
Merlot

VINTNER'S CHOICES
WHITE: *Chardonnay*
RED: *Cabernet Sauvignon*

**ALEXANDER VALLEY
VINEYARDS
8644 HIGHWAY 128
HEALDSBURG, CA 95448
(707) 433-7209**

HOURS: *10 a.m.–5 p.m. daily*
TASTINGS: *Yes*
CHARGE FOR TASTING: *No*
TOURS: *By appointment*
PICNIC AREA: *Yes*
RETAIL SALES: *Yes*

DIRECTIONS: *From Highway
101, drive east on Dry Creek Road.
Turn left on Healdsburg Avenue,
then right on Alexander Valley
Road (becomes Highway 128) for
six miles to winery drive on left.*

FIELD STONE WINERY

Healdsburg

Unlike most conventional wineries built from the ground up, Field Stone was built from the ground down. The late Wallace Johnson chose a natural, oak-studded knoll on his ranch and in the mid-1970s proceeded to carve out a long, narrow slice of earth.

After lining the walls with concrete and building a ceiling, workers redistributed soil over the bunker, returning the knoll to a reasonable facsimile of its former self. The fieldstone used to construct the façade was unearthed during excavation. This intriguing underground facility is said to be the first known winery of its kind built in California since 1900.

Wallace, an inventor of portable aluminum scaffolding, originally had other intentions for this beautiful spot. He had purchased the property in 1955 to pursue an interest in raising purebred cattle.

However, after soil tests a few years later showed the ranch to be well suited to grapevines, Redwood Hereford Ranch evolved into Redwood Ranch and Vineyard. Construction of Field Stone came on the heels of an auspicious planting effort that began in the mid-sixties.

Unfortunately, the rancher-turned-vintner lived to see few crushes. Wallace died in 1979, and the winery passed to his daughter, Katrina, and son-in-law, John Staten.

Although Katrina had become familiar with the business while handling the books for many years, John was pursuing an unrelated career in theological education. Redirecting his efforts, he eagerly set out to earn his new titles of vintner and general manager.

Over the years Field Stone has become well known, earning national attention for its Cabernet Sauvignon and Petite Sirah. The enticing aromas of these and other aging and fermenting wines are evident as visitors navigate rows of barrels toward what has been described as one of the most hospitable tasting rooms in the region. Outside, a number of shaded picnic tables are set up under the oaks.

The old barn on the Field Stone property, now used for storage, was the site of the Alexander Valley's first winery, and the adjacent Petite Sirah vines date back to the late 1800s.

THE WINE LIST
Sauvignon Blanc
Chardonnay
Gewurztraminer
Cabernet Sauvignon
Petite Sirah

VINTNER'S CHOICES
WHITE: *Chardonnay*
RED: *Cabernet Sauvignon*

FIELD STONE WINERY
10075 HIGHWAY 128
HEALDSBURG, CA 95448
(707) 433-7266

HOURS: *10 a.m.–5 p.m. daily*
TASTINGS: *Yes*
CHARGE FOR TASTING: *No*
TOURS: *By appointment*
PICNIC AREA: *Yes*
RETAIL SALES: *Yes*

DIRECTIONS: *From Highway 101, drive east on Dry Creek Road. Turn left on Healdsburg Avenue and right on Alexander Valley Road (becomes Highway 128) to winery drive on right. Winery is near the intersection of Highway 128 and Chalk Hill Road.*

Napa to Clear Lake

To Middletown

CHÂTEAU
MONTELENA ▾

Tubbs Lane
● Calistoga

▾ ROBT.
KEENAN
WINERY

Spring
Mtn.
Rd.

CHÂTEAU
WOLTNER

Deer Park Rd.

▾
DEER
PARK
WINERY

Howell Mtn. Rd.

● St. Helena

29

Silverado Trail

Oakville Grade ● Oakville

CHÂTEAU
POTELLE ▾

Mt. Veeder
Rd.

MAYACAMAS
VINEYARDS ▾

● Yountville

Redwood Rd

HESS ▾
COLLECTION

Napa

Redwood Rd Trancas St.

29

CARNEROS ▾
CREEK WINERY

12

CARNEROS CREEK WINERY

Napa

ack in the early 1970s, when partners Francis Mahoney and Balfour Gibson built the Napa area's first winery since Prohibition in the then-uncharted region known as Carneros, the experts warned that the area was best suited for cattle and masochists. Today, vines greatly outnumber livestock in the Carneros, and neither Francis nor Balfour is suffering.

In fact, the Carneros has since emerged as a prominent grape-growing region, cooled by breezes off San Pablo Bay. Although the region's rocky clay loam reduces yield, it produces unusually high-quality grapes, especially Pinot Noir and Chardonnay.

As winemaker at Carneros Creek, Francis has long been focused on the goal of producing the perfect Pinot Noir. Along the way he enlisted the University of California to assist in determining which clonal selections would produce a Pinot Noir equal in quality to or possibly even better than those of Burgundy. Out of twenty clones, Francis chose six for production.

Today, fifty-five acres of the varietal surround the ivy-covered winery and another ten acres are planted near the Mahoney family home down the road. Additional grapes from other selected vineyards enable the winery to produce about twenty thousand cases per year. The winery also makes smaller amounts of Chardonnay.

In addition to current vintages, the winery offers a library of older wines that during our visit dated all the way back to the 1970s. Those who make the trek out of Napa to visit Carneros Creek Winery are welcome to use picnic tables under the limbs of a sprawling fig tree. The quiet Carneros is as perfect for picnics as it is for Pinot grapes.

THE WINE LIST
Pinot Noir Fleur de Carneros
Pinot Noir Los Carneros
Pinot Noir Signature Reserve,
   available primarily at
   the winery
Chardonnay
Cabernet Sauvignon (library
   selections)

VINTNER'S CHOICES
WHITE: *Chardonnay*
RED: *Pinot Noir Los Carneros*

CARNEROS CREEK WINERY
1285 DEALY LANE
NAPA, CA 94559
(707) 253-9463

HOURS: *9:30 a.m. - 4:30 p.m. daily*
TASTINGS: *Yes*
CHARGE FOR TASTING: *$2; refundable with purchase*
TOURS: *By appointment*
PICNIC AREA: *Yes*
RETAIL SALES: *Yes*

DIRECTIONS: *From Highway 29 south of Napa, take Highway 12 west about three miles. Turn right on Old Sonoma Road (Mont St. John Winery is on the corner), take the first left at Dealy Lane, and drive to winery on left.*

MAYACAMAS VINEYARDS

Napa

One of the region's original backroad wineries, Mayacamas Vineyards sits high in the Mayacamas mountains, separating Napa and Sonoma valleys. The venerable stone winery and its vineyards sit on an ancient volcanic ledge whose rich soil has fed the vines since German-born sword engraver John Fisher established his winemaking operation here in 1889.

Bob Travers, a former San Francisco stock analyst, bought the winery with his wife, Nonie, in 1968. The Travers, who live here in a striking contemporary home, have preserved the adjacent winery's historic appearance.

Like many wineries of its day, Mayacamas was built into the side of a hill (within the ancient volcano's crater) to take advantage of gravity. The uppermost floor contains the crusher and press. From there the juices flow into lined concrete fermentation tanks.

Nature isn't kind to grapevines that grow in this mountain range. Heavy winter rains, poor soil, and rapid drainage stress the vines and

result in small berries. However, these little grapes pack an intense, concentrated flavor that gives the wine a fruity, well-balanced character.

Cabernets are aged in large American oak and small French oak barrels in the old stone-walled cellar. Bob's winemaking techniques ensure longevity for Mayacamas Cabernets, best enjoyed after several years of aging. "We make our red wine this way primarily, of course, to test the patience and restraint of our customers," quipped Bob.

Patience is also required of those who venture up the mountain to the winery. After navigating the eight-or-so miles of winding roads from Napa, visitors — and their vehicles — must endure a mile-long dirt drive before reaching this picturesque estate.

THE WINE LIST
Chardonnay
Sauvignon Blanc
Pinot Noir
Cabernet Sauvignon

VINTNER'S CHOICES:
WHITE: *Chardonnay*
RED: *Cabernet Sauvignon*

MAYACAMAS VINEYARDS
1155 LOKOYA ROAD
NAPA, CA 94558
(707) 224-4030

HOURS: *By appointment only 8 a.m.–4 p.m. Monday through Friday*
TASTINGS: *With tour*
CHARGE FOR TASTING: *No*
TOURS: *By appointment*
PICNIC AREA: *No*
RETAIL SALES: *Yes*

DIRECTIONS: *From Highway 29 in Napa, drive west on Redwood Road (at Redwood Road/Trancas intersection). Redwood Road ultimately becomes Mt. Veeder Road. Follow to top of mountain and turn left on Lokoya Road. Follow Lokoya for a half-mile and turn left just after the mailbox cluster onto the winery drive. Follow for one mile to winery.*

HESS COLLECTION

Napa

The traditional vintner's art mingles with contemporary fine art at the Hess Collection, a bold celebration of art and wine hidden away in the hills above the bustle of Napa Valley.

Don't expect a small, rustic, mom-and-pop operation. This is a stylishly stunning estate where an impressive art collection, a working winery, and a historic limestone cellar have been fused to create a one-of-a-kind backroad wine-country experience. If you have only enough time to visit one Napa area winery, the Hess Collection is our recommended destination.

The founder, Swiss-born entrepreneur Donald Hess, was originally trained as a ninth-generation brewmaster. In addition to taking on

responsibility for his family's brewery and hotel businesses at an early age, Donald founded Valser St. Petersquelle, one of Switzerland's most successful mineral water brands. His holding company, based in Bern, now directs international real estate ventures, cattle ranching, restaurants, resorts, and a line of fruit juice – based soft drinks.

He began creating the Mt. Veeder estate in 1978, expanding the vineyards from around 50 acres to 285. Production currently stands at around twenty-five thousand cases per year, although capacity is eighty thousand cases.

The 1903-vintage, three-story stone winery, the first Napa Valley winery of the Christian Brothers, serves as cornerstone of the estate. After two years of extensive renovation, the winery opened as the Hess Collection in 1989. The cellar is the first stop on the self-guided tour.

It's here that the Hess wines, sealed in French oak barrels, age in cool darkness. One of Donald's chief goals has been to create wines that are drinkable on release but that age well for years. Hess Chardonnays, which typically remain in the barrel about ten months, and Cabernet Sauvignons, which age for nearly two years, have received impressive reviews from critics.

The upper floors of the old stone building have been transformed to house more than 125 pieces of art representing more than twenty years of collecting by Donald and his wife, Joanna. Included are paintings and sculpture — many of them profoundly affecting — produced since 1960 by European and American artists.

At various locations, interior windows have been cut in the walls to frame views into the winery. From the third-floor landing, for example, the tops of stainless steel fermenting tanks are visible through a large porthole. The bottling line can be studied from another corner.

Visitors may sample the Hess wines in an elegant tasting room that once was a sherry production facility. There is a charge for tasting but no admission fee.

THE WINE LIST
Chardonnay
Cabernet Sauvignon
Cabernet Sauvignon Reserve

VINTNER'S CHOICES
WHITE: *Hess Collection Napa Valley Chardonnay*
RED: *Hess Collection Cabernet Sauvignon*

HESS COLLECTION
4411 REDWOOD ROAD
P.O. BOX 4140
NAPA, CA 94558
(707) 255-1144

HOURS: *10 a.m.– 4 p.m. daily*
TASTINGS: *Yes*
CHARGE FOR TASTING: *Yes*
TOURS: *Self-guided*
PICNIC AREA: *No*
RETAIL SALES: *Yes*

DIRECTIONS: *From Highway 29 in Napa (at Redwood Road/Trancas intersection), drive west on Redwood Road for six miles to winery on left.*

CHÂTEAU POTELLE

Napa

*D*on't be fooled by the Napa address of the Fourmeaux du Sartel family winery. Napa proper seemed a million miles away as we made our way up the mountainside from Oakville to the lofty reaches of Mt. Veeder. In this remote setting, Jean-Noel and Marketta Fourmeaux du Sartel, interrupted only by the occasional visitor, quietly practice winemaking skills expertly honed in Bordeaux.

When we stopped by, not a soul was in sight, and a sign on the tasting-room door suggested that visitors honk their horn to alert family members busy elsewhere on the grounds.

This scenic property, whose inhabitants also include squirrels, deer, and an occasional bear or mountain lion, was known for several years as Vose Vineyards. Jean-Noel and Marketta, former official winetasters for the French government, left those enviable roles in 1987 to buy the estate, which they operate with help from daughters Marietta and

Clarisse. They renamed the winery after the family's nine-hundred-year-old château in the Champagne region. The Fourmeaux du Sartels still own châteaux in Bordeaux and make several trips each year to their homeland.

Tastings at Château Potelle are conducted in a tiny cottage your visit be sure to ask for a taste of Château Potelle's stylish Zinfandel, which has turned more than a few heads since the first release of the varietal in 1990.

An attractive stone-walled winery stands just downslope, adjacent to rolling vineyards. Although the winery isn't open for tours, guests are invited to linger on the deck, where a gazebo and tables command views of the vineyards, forest, and rugged mountains. A call in advance to reserve a table is requested.

Also noteworthy is the private lane leading from Mt. Veeder Road to the winery. What must rank as one of the region's longest driveways meanders up hills and along ridges through some of Napa's most memorable scenery.

THE WINE LIST
Sauvignon Blanc
Chardonnay
Cabernet Sauvignon
Zinfandel

VINTNER'S CHOICES
WHITE: *Sauvignon Blanc*
RED: *Cabernet Sauvignon*

CHÂTEAU POTELLE
3875 MT. VEEDER ROAD
NAPA, CA 94558
(707) 255-9440

HOURS: *11:30 a.m. - 5 p.m. Friday through Monday; closed December through March*
TASTINGS: *Yes*
CHARGE FOR TASTING: *No*
TOURS: *No*
PICNIC AREA: *By appointment*
RETAIL SALES: *Yes*

DIRECTIONS: *From Highway 29 at Oakville, drive west on Oakville Grade for three and one-half miles. Turn left on Mt. Veeder Road and drive two miles to winery sign on right. Follow private lane to winery.*

ROBERT KEENAN WINERY

St. Helena

Since the wine-country tourist crowd rarely ventures more than a mile or two out of St. Helena on Spring Mountain Road, we thought we'd made quite a discovery when we kept driving (past dozens of cars and buses gathered at the popular Spring Mountain Winery) and found ourselves on the gravel road leading to the classic, stone-walled Robert Keenan Winery. Then the tasting-room hostess told us that the winery had been here since the turn of the century. So much for discoveries.

Peter Conradi established these remote vineyards in 1892 and built the winery a dozen years later. However, the vines were ultimately abandoned and the estate deteriorated.

Then along came Robert and Ann Keenan, who reclaimed the site in 1974 from the encroaching forest. Robert replanted nearly fifty acres of Cabernet Sauvignon, Chardonnay, and Merlot and set about completely refurbishing the old winery. The project was completed in time for a 1974 harvest. These days, the Keenans produce fewer than ten thousand cases per year from almost sixty acres.

The Keenan facility is a small, rustically handsome stone building set in a hill below a thick forest. A grand mountain panorama unfolds beyond the adjacent vineyards.

By the way, we found our visit to the Keenan estate well worth the cost of the car wash we needed after leaving this winery's back road.

THE WINE LIST
Chardonnay
Cabernet Franc
Cabernet Sauvignon
Merlot

VINTNER'S CHOICES
WHITE: *Chardonnay*
RED: *Cabernet Sauvigon*

ROBERT KEENAN WINERY
3660 SPRING MOUNTAIN ROAD
ST. HELENA, CA 94574
(707) 963-9177

HOURS: *By appointment only; 8 a.m.–5 p.m., Monday through Friday*
TASTINGS: *Yes*
CHARGE FOR TASTING: *No*
TOURS: *By appointment*
PICNIC AREA: *No*
RETAIL SALES: *Yes*

DIRECTIONS: *From Highway 29 at St. Helena, head west on Madrona Road and drive three blocks to Spring Mountain Road. Turn right and drive four and one-half miles to winery lane. Turn right and follow for nearly one mile to winery.*

DEER PARK WINERY

Deer Park

Whoever said that good things come in small packages must have stopped by Deer Park Winery. One of Napa Valley's smallest winemaking operations — only three thousand cases are produced annually — it's nonetheless one of the region's most charming.

The old winery, which celebrated its centennial in 1991, rises from a gentle hillside at the base of Howell Mountain. Deer Park wines are made the old-fashioned way in the two-story stone building. The crush takes place on the upper level; the juices are then fed by gravity into casks on the ground floor, which is carved into the hill.

Grapes are taken from just over three acres of vines. The remaining forty or so acres on the Deer Park property consist primarily of rocks, hills, and trees — nice to look at, but not conducive to cultivation.

After sitting dormant for nearly twenty years, the estate was purchased in 1979 by winemaker David Clark and his wife, Kinta, along with partners Robert and Lila Knapp. Over the years David has

added new plantings and restored the winery to picture-perfect condition, right down to the weather-vaned cupola.

David and Kinta sell most of their wines through the tasting room and welcome visitors. However, since their duties are numerous, a phone call in advance is requested.

The name indicates otherwise, but the Clarks claim there are no deer at Deer Park. The way David tells it, the winery's moniker was apparently conceived by a 1920s-era owner who wanted to shake any unpleasant association of his winery with the country byway that ends at the property: Sanitarium Road.

THE WINE LIST
Chardonnay
Sauvignon Blanc Late Harvest
Cabernet Sauvignon
Petite Sirah
Zinfandel

VINTNER'S CHOICES
WHITE: *Sauvignon Blanc*
Late Harvest
RED: *Zinfandel Reserve*

DEER PARK WINERY
1000 DEER PARK ROAD
DEER PARK, CA 94576
(707) 963-5411

HOURS: *By appointment only: 10 a.m.–4:30 p.m. Monday through Saturday*
TASTINGS: *By appointment*
CHARGE FOR TASTING: *No*
TOURS: *By appointment*
PICNIC AREA: *By appointment*
RETAIL SALES: *By appointment*

DIRECTIONS: *From Highway 29 or the Silverado Trail north of St. Helena, drive east three miles from Highway 29 on Deer Park Road to winery gate on right.*

CHÂTEAU WOLTNER

Angwin

We thought we'd heard about or seen every winemaking operation in the Napa Valley region until David Clark of Deer Park Winery steered us a bit farther up Howell Mountain to Château Woltner. For those who've grown tired of the same Napa destinations, this magnificent cellar should qualify as a genuine backroad discovery.

No, it's not new. The three-level stone-walled winery was constructed in 1886 by Chinese laborers who came to California to help cut the route of the first transcontinental railway over the Sierra. Operated by two Frenchmen, the Nouveau Medoc Wine Cellars, as it was known in the early days, was the heart of a thriving 190-acre wine estate.

Wine was made at the winery until Prohibition, after which bulk wines were made sporadically for a short time. The old cellar

languished from 1946 until 1980, when Francis and Francoise DeWavrin-Woltner sold their Bordeaux estate and bought the Howell Mountain property. The couple invested some $7 million and more than five years to restore the winery and to replant old and establish new vineyards. Their first crush wasn't until 1985.

Wine is made here using a method similar to that followed by early winemakers. Grapes are hauled to the crusher through doors on the top level. Juices from the crushed grapes flow into vats and barrels situated

on the lower levels, which are notched into the hillside. The lowest floor is completely buried on three sides. Two-and-a-half-foot-thick stone walls keep the cellar at a consistently cool sixty degrees.

The Woltners make five kinds of Chardonnay from carefully selected grapes. While in 1990 the average Chardonnay production in Napa Valley was 4.64 tons per acre, Château Woltner's yield was only 1.61 tons per acre.

Because of the comparatively low yields and the extreme precision with which the grapes are handled, one of Château Woltner's Chardonnays — from the Frederique Vineyard — ranks among California's most expensive. At the time of our visit, the more limited wines were priced from around $26 to nearly $60 per bottle. However, Château Woltner's impressive Howell Mountain version was selling for around $12 per bottle.

THE WINE LIST
Chardonnay

VINTNER'S CHOICE
WHITE: *Frederique Vineyard Chardonnay*

CHÂTEAU WOLTNER
150 SOUTH WHITE COTTAGE ROAD
ANGWIN, CA 94508
(707) 965-2445

HOURS: *By appointment only: 8 a.m.–4 p.m. Monday through Friday*
TASTINGS: *By appointment*
CHARGE FOR TASTING: *No*
TOURS: *By appointment*
PICNIC AREA: *No*
RETAIL SALES: *Yes*

DIRECTIONS: *From Highway 29 north of St. Helena, head east on Deer Park Road. One mile past Burgess Cellars, turn left on White Cottage Road (there's no sign) and drive 1.2 miles to mail box (150 White Cottage Road) on left.*

CHÂTEAU MONTELENA

Calistoga

Some critics might quibble about whether Château Montelena qualifies for backroad status, but this wine estate tucked among trees off Tubbs Lane is our favorite Napa Valley winery to visit. It's also the only destination we've included from the valley itself.

The château was built in 1882 by California state senator and prominent Bay Area businessman Alfred Tubbs. In establishing his winery near the base of Mount St. Helena, Senator Tubbs called upon the design talents of an architect from France, who created a building

in the style of a French château. The medieval façade (you'll need to walk around back to see it) was fashioned from imported cut stone. The other walls — the winery is cut into the side of a hill — are as thick as twelve feet in certain places, providing a cavelike climate.

While the winery itself conjures up images of feudal Bordeaux, the adjacent grounds look as though they've been lifted from a garden in Beijing. Jade Lake, with its delicate teahouses, gracefully intricate bridges, and an old Chinese junk, was added to the property by the Yort Franks, previous owners who in the 1950s created a living reminder of their Chinese homeland.

The latest chapter in the Château Montelena story is being written by a partnership that took over in 1972. The owners have preserved

the architectural integrity of the winery and nurtured the gardens while carving out a positive reputation for their product. This is evidenced partially in framed menus from the White House that list Montelena wines. (Château Montelena's Chardonnay was said to be Nancy Reagan's favorite.) This memorabilia hangs in the tasting room, along with other awards bestowed on the château's wines in recent years.

THE WINE LIST
Chardonnay
Johannisberg Riesling
Zinfandel
Cabernet Sauvignon

VINTNER'S CHOICES
WHITE: *Chardonnay*
RED: *Cabernet Sauvignon*

CHÂTEAU MONTELENA
1429 TUBBS LANE
CALISTOGA, CA 94515
(707) 942-5105

HOURS: *10 a.m.–4 p.m.*
TASTINGS: *Yes*
CHARGE FOR TASTING: *Yes*
TOURS: *By appointment*
PICNIC AREA: *By appointment*
RETAIL SALES: *Yes*

DIRECTIONS: *From Highway 128 two miles north of Calistoga, drive one and one-half miles east on Tubbs Lane to winery gate on left. From Highway 29, drive west on Tubbs Lane for one-quarter mile to winery gate on right.*

GUENOC ESTATE VINEYARDS AND WINERY

Middletown

Many visitors to this sprawling winemaking operation are surprised to learn that the mysterious-looking beauty whose visage appears on the label is not only the famous late actress Lillie Langtry, but that "Jersey Lily," as she became known, is the winery's original proprietor.

The popular stage actress, who performed internationally during the late nineteenth and early twentieth centuries, called the Guenoc Valley home for a time. It was here, at the northern tip of Napa Valley, that Lillie renovated a stately two-story home. She bought the estate in 1888 and owned it for nearly twenty years. In 1891, fifty tons of grapes were crushed on her property. Most of Lillie's wine was marketed in barrels, although some bottles with labels bearing her famous likeness were sold. The first vines here were planted in 1854.

Brothers Orville and Bob Magoon acquired the estate in 1963 in exchange for property on the island of Oahu. Bob is a Broadway musical writer; Orville is Guenoc's winegrower and was responsible for the development of the estate which encompasses some twenty-three thousand acres. The estate is the nation's first single-proprietor viticultural appellation.

Between ninety and one-hundred thousand cases are produced every year by the Magoon family. The winery also bottles a limited quantity under the Domaine Breton label.

Although Lillie Langtry's historic home isn't on the public tour, it is visible in the distance and is open once each

year in May. Visitors may tour the winery, an attractive, hospitable tasting room, and grounds that include a long, trellis-covered picnic area overlooking a small lake.

THE WINE LIST
Chardonnay
Chardonnay Reserve
Sauvignon Blanc
Chenin Blanc
Semillon
Langtry Meritage White
Langtry Meritage Red
Zinfandel
Domaine Breton Zinfandel
Cabernet Sauvignon
Petite Sirah
Merlot

VINTNER'S CHOICES
WHITE: *Genevieve Magoon*
    Reserve Chardonnay
RED: *Langtry Meritage Red*

GUENOC ESTATE
VINEYARDS AND WINERY
21000 BUTTS CANYON ROAD
MIDDLETOWN, CA 95461
(707) 987-2385

HOURS: *10 a.m.– 4:30 p.m.*
Thursday through Sunday
TASTINGS: *Yes*
CHARGE FOR TASTING: *No*
TOURS: *Yes*
PICNIC AREA: *Yes*
RETAIL SALES: *Yes*

DIRECTIONS: *From Highway 29 at Middletown, north of Calistoga, drive east on Butts Canyon Road for six and one-half miles.*

Winters to St. Helena

128

▼ NICHELINI
WINERY

128

WINTERS
WINERY ▼

Silverado Trail

121

505

Napa

▼ WOODEN VALLEY
WINERY

To
Sacramento

80

To San Francisco

WINTERS WINERY

Winters

*T*he University of California, Davis, has trained many of California's top vintners, but most graduates move on to practice their craft in regions more famous for winemaking. David Storm set up shop just a few miles away in the sleepy little town of Winters.

David, who holds bachelor's, master's, and doctorate degrees from the University of California, Davis, founded Winters Winery in 1980, after working as a consulting civil and sanitary engineer. In addition to serving as a consultant to wineries on water and waste-water problems, he made wine at home for more than a decade before starting his commercial venture.

He chose a downtown Winters landmark that since 1876 has housed a general store, butcher, baker, and a turn-of-the-century opera house and dining room. In contrast to the previous tenants, David was attracted by the building's thick brick walls and cellar, which he found well-suited for winemaking.

Not only has the three-story building proved to be a functional space for a wine production facility, it's an appealing place to linger over a sample or two. Visitors are welcomed into a high-ceilinged room that has been attractively refitted for tastings and retail sales. David has furnished this public room with antique furniture and winemaking equipment. The street-level rooms also contain a laboratory and areas for fermenting and case storage. Aging takes place in the cellar.

Assisted by sons Tyghe and Todd, David produces between one and five thousand cases per year. Syrah and Petite Sirah grapes are grown on a six-acre vineyard in the Olive School sector of Solano County and from vines in other parts of the north state. During the time of my visit, Winters Winery was not producing white wines.

THE WINE LIST
Petite Sirah
Syrah
Zinfandel

VINTNER'S CHOICE
RED: *Petite Sirah*

WINTERS WINERY
15 MAIN STREET
WINTERS, CA 95694
(916) 795-3201

HOURS: *By appointment: 10 a.m.–5 p.m. Monday through Friday*
TASTINGS: *By appointment*
CHARGE FOR TASTING: *By appointment*
TOURS: *By appointment*
PICNIC AREA: *No*
RETAIL SALES: *Yes*

DIRECTIONS: *From Interstate 80, drive north on Interstate 505 for twelve miles to Winters/Highway 128 exit. Turn left off the freeway exit ramp onto Railroad Avenue, drive four blocks to Main Street and turn right. Winery is on the right. For Napa Valley–bound travelers using Interstate 80 out of Davis, the Highway 128 route via Winters and over the mountains to Rutherford is a scenic backroad alternative to the traditional drive along Highway 12 to Highway 29. Rutherford is forty miles from Winters.*

WOODEN VALLEY WINERY

Suisun

Wooden Valley Vineyards is only about ten miles from Napa as the crow flies. Because of the mountain range that separates the Napa and Suisun valleys, however, few wine-country tourists ever make it to the eastern side of the hills.

One of the few "other side" winemaking operations is Wooden Valley Winery, a family-run business situated along the winding road that ultimately connects with Highway 121 out of Napa.

Whenever I stop by, loyal customers — most of them locals — pull

up, exchange pleasantries with one or more of the Lanza family members, and load their vehicles with Wooden Valley wines. While the product is available at a couple of stores, about 90 percent of Wooden Valley wines are sold out of the tasting room.

Wooden Valley has been supplying Solano County residents with wine since the late Mario Lanza (no relation to the singer) bought more than 150 acres of fruit trees and refocused the property on grapes. Mario's son, Richard (known locally as Chick) Lanza, who later assumed the lead role, is now assisted by his sons, Ron, Rick, Ken, and Larry. Richard's wife, Adrienne, also helps out at the winery, as does Mario's widow, Lena, who fixes daily lunches for the hard-working family.

The winery compound consists of a tasting room large enough to hold supplies of nearly twenty different wines, the Lanza home, and the winery. Owned and leased vineyards totaling 350 acres supply grapes for some twenty-five thousand cases per year.

THE WINE LIST
Chardonnay
Sauvignon Blanc
Johannisberg Riesling
White Zinfandel
Gewurztraminer
Chenin Blanc
Petite Rosé
Cabernet Sauvignon
Merlot
Chianti
Gamay Beaujolais
Zinfandel
Chablis
Rhine
Haut Sauterne
Vino Bianco
Golden Chateau
Burgundy
Vino Rosso

VINTNER'S CHOICES
WHITE: *Chardonnay*
RED: *Merlot*

WOODEN VALLEY WINERY
4756 SUISUN VALLEY ROAD
SUISUN, CA 94585
(707) 864-0730

HOURS: *9 a.m.–5 p.m., Tuesday through Sunday*
TASTINGS: *Yes*
CHARGE FOR TASTING: *No*
TOURS: *No*
PICNIC AREA: *Yes*
RETAIL SALES: *Yes*

DIRECTIONS: *From Interstate 80 at Cordelia, drive north on Suisun Valley Road for five miles to winery on right.*

NICHELINI WINERY

St. Helena

There may be safety in numbers, but Antone Nichelini, the Swiss-Italian patriarch of the Napa region's longest continuously operated family winery, chose to go his own way. At the time he homesteaded some land along Sage Canyon Road and built a small winery, the closest winemaking establishment was miles away in Napa Valley.

It was back in 1890 that the founder built the sandstone-walled winery and topped it with a modest home, where he raised a family.

Many of Nichelini's customers were Italian emigrants who worked the local magnesite mines.

The operation outlived the region's mining industry and thrived until Prohibition, during which the elder Nichelini was accused of maintaining a clandestine winemaking business. Unable to obtain a license upon Repeal, Antone passed the operation to his son, William.

More than one hundred years after that first crush, Nichelini descendants still make wine here. A harvest-time visit found Dick

Wainright, Antone's grandson, working the bottling line with his wife, Dolores, as well as Joe and Carol Nichelini. Antone's great-grandson, Greg Boeger, who owns his own winery in Placerville (see separate listing), serves as winemaker.

With the exception of a few contemporary additions that make the winemaking process more efficient, the property retains a vintage look. Displayed behind the tasting bar is a century-old Roman press, which was retired in the 1950s. It's thought to be among very few such relics in the western world.

Because the family members who run the winery have other business commitments, the winery is only open Saturday and Sunday. During the weekends, the Nichelini clan gathers to handcraft three estate red varietals. Greg Boeger supplies his own foothill-made white wines.

The East Bay

580

Livermore

S. Livermore
Ave.

▼ CHOUINARD
VINEYARDS

Stanley
Blvd.

▼ RETZLAFF
VINEYARDS

L
St.

▼ CONCANNON
VINEYARDS

Palomares
Rd.

Holmes St.

Tesla Rd.

Mines Rd.

▼ ELLISTON
VINEYARDS

FENESTRA
WINERY ▼

Kilkare Rd.

84

Niles Canyon Rd.
(Sunol Exit)

Wetmore Rd.

MURRIETA'S
WELL ▼

680

To San Jose

CHOUINARD VINEYARDS

Castro Valley

Thanks to Northern California's temperate climate, it's increasingly difficult to find an area not conducive to growing at least a few varieties of grapes. From the San Joaquin Valley to the Mendocino coast, the wine industry continues to thrive. In 1985, with the bonding of tiny Chouinard Vineyard and Winery, Palomares Canyon was added to the expanding list of north state winemaking areas.

The circumstances that led to the establishment of this family-run winery were set in motion in the early 1970s, when architect George Chouinard (shin-ARD) was appointed to head the Parisian office of his international construction engineering firm. During their two-year stay in Chavenay, France, George, his wife, Caroline, and then-teenaged sons Rick and Damian became acquainted with the winemaking operations of the Champagne district.

Returning stateside in 1976, George was presented with an attractive offer to head his company's international operations unit, a

THE WINE LIST
Chardonnay
Livermore Semillon
Gewurztraminer
Johannisberg Riesling
Chenin Blanc
Granny Smith Apple
Cabernet Sauvignon

VINTNER'S CHOICES
WHITE: *Granny Smith Apple*
RED: *Cabernet Sauvignon*

CHOUINARD VINEYARDS
33853 PALOMARES CANYON ROAD
CASTRO VALLEY, CA 94552
(415) 582-9900

HOURS: *12 p.m.–5 p.m. Saturday, Sunday, and some holidays*
TASTINGS: *Yes*
CHARGE FOR TASTING: *No*
TOURS: *By request*
PICNIC AREA: *Yes*
RETAIL SALES: *Yes*

DIRECTIONS: *From Highway 580, take the Palomares/Eden Canyon exit and drive one-quarter mile. Turn south on Palo Verde Road and turn left on Palomares Canyon Road. Drive six miles to winery on right. From Highway 680, take the Sunol exit and drive west along Niles Canyon Road to Palomares Canyon Road. Turn right and follow five miles to winery on left.*

Continued next page

promotion that would have required the Chouinards to relocate to Chicago. Instead, George reassessed his priorities and resigned, purchasing 110 acres high in the hills that separate San Francisco Bay from Livermore Valley.

George and Caroline began making wine (two hundred cases) in 1985, but it wasn't until Damian graduated from Fresno State University's enology program in 1987 that the business really began to

take off. By the following year Chouinard was producing nearly two thousand cases.

Because much of the family's property is steep, the vineyards here were originally confined to the level, three-acre site of a former corral. Several acres of terraced vines were planted in 1990. The Chouinards are also encouraging neighbors to plant vineyards in order to increase the region's grape output.

Visitors are received on the second-level tasting area of a half-century-old redwood barn that George, aided by Rick, a carpenter and electrician, converted into a winery. A rear deck looks out over the vineyards and into the hills. Fermentation tanks and barrels take up the ground level. The Chouinards use a portable bottling operation.

One of the Chouinards' most popular wares is a distinctive, tart, and dry Granny Smith Apple Wine made from Paso Robles area apples.

ELLISTON VINEYARDS

Sunol

The beautiful estate now producing wines under the Elliston label endured some rough times before schoolteachers Ray and Amy Awtrey rescued the neglected property in 1969. While the sturdy old mansion was restorable, the estate's mature-but-decaying three-acre vineyard, which had produced wine grapes until Prohibition, wasn't so lucky.

After rebonding the winemaking operation in 1982, the Awtreys leased a nearby fifty-five-acre vineyard from the San Francisco Water Department and replanted their own plot to Chardonnay grapes. The leased property includes what the Awtreys believe are the state's only Pinot Gris vines.

The magnificent seventeen-room mansion that is the estate's center-piece was built in 1890 as a summer home for shipping and grain magnate and onetime San Francisco police chief Henry Hiram Ellis.

Now a registered historic landmark, the four-story home was made from locally quarried blue sandstone.

The adjacent oak-shaded winery that sits against Pleasanton Ridge served originally as the estate's carriage house. Tastings are conducted at an informal bar just inside the massive double doors. The rear portion of the building extends into the hill and thus provides a cool resting place for aging Elliston's vintages. The production facility is in Felton in the Santa Cruz mountains.

Among the four wines produced by winemaker Dan Gehrs is an award-winning blend of Chardonnay, Pinot Blanc, and Pinot Gris.

The tasting room draws a few passersby on Saturday and Sunday, but the majority of visitors who make their way up scenic Kilkare Road are guests of the many weddings and private parties held here.

THE WINE LIST
Chardonnay
Pinot Blanc
Pinot Gris
*Blend of the above three wines
  also available*

VINTNER'S CHOICE:
WHITE: *Chardonnay*

ELLISTON VINEYARDS
463 KILKARE ROAD
SUNOL, CA 94586
(415) 862-2377

HOURS: *Weekdays by appointment only; weekends from 12 p.m.–4 p.m.*

TASTINGS: *Yes*
CHARGE FOR TASTING: *No*
TOURS: *No*
PICNIC AREA: *Yes*
RETAIL SALES: *Yes*

DIRECTIONS: *From south-bound Highway 680, take Highway 84 (exit is marked Sunol/Calaveras/Dumbarton Bridge). Drive through the first intersection and make a quick right turn onto Main Street, Sunol. At the end of Main Street, turn right on Kilkare Road and drive a half-mile to winery on right. From eastbound Niles Canyon Road (Highway 84), take the Sunol exit (on right before tunnel). From Main Street, take the first left turn onto Kilkare Road and drive a half-mile to winery on right.*

FENESTRA WINERY

Livermore

Our favorite Livermore Valley winery is a weather-beaten old barn now being given new life by two energetic locals. Fenestra Winery, owned and operated by the husband-wife team of Lanny and Fran Replogle of nearby Sunol, is a veritable working wine museum.

The rustic structure had not been used as a winery for two decades when Lanny and Fran decided to leave their smaller digs in the old Ruby Hills Winery in 1980. The Replogles and their two sons spent the better part of a year hauling away tons of trash, rehabilitating the structure, and adding a few modern winemaking conveniences. Still, little appears to have changed here since George and Christiana True built the winery in 1889.

Lanny, who holds a Ph.D. in organic chemistry from the University of Washington, started making wines at home in the early 1960s, about the same time he became a chemistry professor at San Jose State University. He stepped into the commercial wine industry in the early

1970s, spending three summer vacations working on experimental grape-crushing techniques in the Paul Masson Winery's research department. Lanny began making his own wine commercially at Stony Ridge in 1976.

The Fenestra site has no vineyards, so Lanny hits the wine roads each fall in search of grapes. His favorite locales are Livermore Valley, Napa Valley, and Monterey County. Fenestra's acclaimed Monterey County Cabernet Sauvignon comes from grapes grown at Smith and Hook Vineyards in the Santa Lucia mountains.

During the cold and rainy months, the Replogles pour their wines at an indoor tasting bar. When the sun is out, visitors are received on the adjacent patio under an old walnut tree.

Many of those who drop by are members of Fenestra Fanatics, the name given to the Replogles' wine club. Members receive two bottles — chosen by the owners — each quarter. The couple also hosts a series of special tastings of new releases and special food creations.

THE WINE LIST
Chardonnay
Semillon
Pinot Blanc
Sauvignon Blanc
White Riesling
White Zinfandel
True Red, a Zinfandel and
    Ruby Cabernet blend
Zinfandel
Merlot
Cabernet Sauvignon

VINTNER'S CHOICES
WHITE: *Semillon*
RED: *Merlot*

FENESTRA WINERY
83 EAST VALLECITOS ROAD
LIVERMORE, CA
(510) 862-2292
MAILING ADDRESS:
2954 KILKARE ROAD
SUNOL, CA 94586

HOURS: *12 p.m.–5 p.m.*
Saturday and Sunday
TASTINGS: *Yes*
CHARGE FOR TASTING: *No*
TOURS: *By appointment*
PICNIC AREA: *Yes*
RETAIL SALES: *Yes*

DIRECTIONS: *From northbound Highway 680, exit east at the Livermore/Highway 84 exit and drive six miles to winery on left. From southbound Highway 680, exit at Junction 84 and turn left under freeway to Calaveras sign. Turn right at Vallecitos Road (briefly back onto Highway 680) and take Livermore/Highway 84 exit. Drive east six miles to winery on left.*

MURRIETA'S WELL

Livermore

*L*egendary bandit Joaquin Murrieta was apparently among the first to recognize the potential of this scenic ranch, located on the outskirts of Livermore. According to local accounts, Joaquin regarded water from a well on the property as the best around and made regular stops here to rest and water his horses.

In the early 1880s, Murrieta's well, as it came to be known, nourished the fledgling vineyard of winemaker Louis Mel, who also constructed the stone winery. Louis and fellow vintner Charles Wetmore imported high-quality European cuttings of Semillon, Sauvignon Vert, Sauvignon Blanc, and Muscadelle de Bordelais and went on to earn international

recognition for their wines. Louis and Charles, who later provided cuttings to other Livermore Valley growers, are regarded among this wine region's most important pioneers.

In 1930 the Mel wine estate was purchased by the Wente family, which continued to cultivate and improve the vineyards over the next sixty years. Then, in 1990, Philip Wente joined forces with Sergio Traverso to restore the old stone winery. Sergio, who holds a Ph.D. in microbiology from the University of California, Davis, divides his time between the Livermore Valley property and his native Chile, where he makes Cabernet Sauvignon and Merlot, which is imported to the United States.

Although the winery produces four types of wine, its Vendimia Red and Vendimia White blends earn the highest praise. Vendimia White (first released in 1992) is a blend of Sauvignon Blanc and Semillon,

with a discreet amount of Muscat de Frontignan (Muscat Canelli) grapes. Vendimia Red (first released in 1993) is made from Cabernet Sauvignon, Merlot, and Cabernet Franc.

Visitors who inquire at Murrieta's Well about Joaquin will hear a story that is at variance with popular legend. Winery literature describes Joaquin Murrieta as a man whose family was savagely murdered not long after coming to California from Mexico during the gold rush. His anger manifested in a vengeance that quickly became the stuff of legend, but many crimes attributed to him were likely perpetrated by at least five other *bandidos* named Joaquin who were operating throughout California. Eluding capture, Joaquin supposedly became the leader of an expert band of horsemen that rounded up wild horses and sold them in Sonora, Mexico. A horseman's spur served as inspiration for the winery's logo.

THE WINE LIST
Chardonnay
Vendimia White
Vendimia Red
Zinfandel

VINTNER'S CHOICES
WHITE: *Vendimia White*
RED: *Vendimia Red*

MURRIETA'S WELL
3005 MINES ROAD
LIVERMORE VALLEY, CA 94550
(510) 449-9239

HOURS: *10 a.m.– 4 p.m. Saturday and Sunday*
TASTINGS: *Yes*
CHARGE FOR TASTING: *No*
TOURS: *By appointment*
PICNIC AREA: *No*
RETAIL SALES: *Yes*

DIRECTIONS: *From Highway 580, exit at Livermore Avenue and drive south to Tesla Road, which veers left. At Mines Road (past Concannon), turn right and drive to mailbox marked 3005. Turn right on lane that leads to winery.*

CONCANNON VINEYARD

Livermore

James Concannon's pioneering efforts in the western wine industry were at least partially the result of urgings from a San Francisco archbishop who needed a reliable source of sacramental wines for the Catholic Church. The Irish immigrant obliged in 1883 by establishing what is today one of the state's oldest continuously operating wineries.

James transcended the original intention of his winery, becoming well known internationally. In searching for other grape-growing

locales, he later took his talents to Mexico and is widely credited with establishing that country's wine industry.

The winery still produces sacramental wines but is better known these days for such varietals as Chardonnay and Cabernet Sauvignon. Concannon made news in 1964 by becoming the first American winery to make a varietal wine from Petite Sirah.

Although the winery was owned during the 1980s by European firms, James Concannon's grandson, Jim, remained with the business. Concannon was purchased in 1992 by a partnership that includes members of the famous winemaking Wente family.

A cavernous masonry facility that sits amid vinelands at the edge of Livermore, the winery makes admirable efforts to accommodate visitors. Tours are given four times daily, and the tasting room is open

seven days a week. Concannon's well-maintained grounds include a sprawling tree-shaded lawn with several picnic tables and a gazebo.

THE WINE LIST
Sauvignon Blanc
Chardonnay
Vintage White
White Zinfandel
Johannisberg Riesling
Semillon
Cabernet Sauvignon
Petite Sirah
Vintage Red

VINTNER'S CHOICES
WHITE: *Sauvignon Blanc*
RED: *Petite Sirah*

CONCANNON VINEYARD
4590 TESLA ROAD
LIVERMORE, CA 94550
(510) 447-3760

HOURS: *10 a.m.–4:30 p.m. Monday through Saturday; 12 p.m.–4:30 p.m. Sunday*
TASTINGS: *Yes*
CHARGE FOR TASTING: *No*
TOURS: *Four times daily*
PICNIC AREA: *Yes*
RETAIL SALES: *Yes*

DIRECTIONS: *From Highway 580, take the North Livermore Avenue exit and drive south three miles to Tesla Road, which veers left. Winery is on the left.*

RETZLAFF VINEYARDS

Livermore

In 1979, Robert and Gloria Taylor sold their house in town and moved their family to a thirteen-acre ranch in the country, where they established a vineyard. Since Robert was involved in a career as a research chemist and Gloria was active in civic affairs and as an artist, they sold most of their early crops to the Wente brothers. However, the Taylors saved some of their Grey Riesling grapes and began to experiment as home winemakers. They began selling their wares to the public in 1986. (Retzlaff is Gloria's maiden name.)

Over the years, Livermore has crept to the ranch's edges, but the property still retains a decidedly country atmosphere, thanks to the quaint old home and other restored Victorian farm buildings that serve the winery business. Samples are poured in the little green tasting room, just off a spacious lawn dotted with picnic tables.

Among the most prized of Retzlaff wines are the gold medal–winning Cabernet Sauvignon and a highly rated Merlot, whose aroma is described by Gloria as "a walk in the woods on a foggy morning."

The Retzlaff estate is the site of a number of popular events, including a series of spring, summer, and fall full-moon dinners. Each winter the winery extends invitations to barrel tastings at which futures of still-aging wines are sold at considerable savings over the ultimate retail price of the wines. Participants are invited back to a spring open house, when the actual bottled wines are made available.

The Coastal Mountains

To San Francisco

To San Francisco

RIDGE VINEYARDS ▼

SUNRISE
WINERY ▼

280

San Jose

1

HALLCREST
VINEYARD

BONNY
DOON ▼

17

101

9

Santa Cruz

Morgan
Hill

▼ BARGETTO WINERY

Watsonville
Rd.

Soquel

SYCAMORE CREEK ▼
VINEYARDS

KIRIGIN
▼ CELLARS

1

FORTINO
WINERY ▼

LIVE OAKS
WINERY ▼

Watsonville

152

Gilroy

Hecker Pass Rd.

To Monterey

SUNRISE WINERY

Cupertino

Approaching the Picchetti ranch winery, I halfway expected to encounter a grizzled old cowboy, a jug or two in hand, heading back to the bunkhouse.

California still holds a few surviving wineries from before the twentieth century. No other, however, retains quite the authentic flavor that has been preserved on this old ranch, located in a surprisingly rustic spot about ten minutes from Apple Computer's headquarters.

Now known as Sunrise Winery, the ranch consists of several vintage buildings, many of which stand in a state of arrested decay. Although the old brick winery has received some restorative treatments over the years, visitors to the wooden-floored tasting room on the second level encounter a scene that appears much like it must have back in the old days. The outbuildings, which include the rickety Picchetti homestead (built in 1876) and the fermentation building (under restoration), also offer an authentic glimpse into another time.

Much like the state's efforts in preserving the gold rush town of Columbia in the Mother Lode, the Midpeninsula Regional Open Space District stepped in to purchase property here on the Monte Bello Ridge of the Santa Cruz mountains back in the mid-1970s and created a 360-acre open-space preserve. The winery and surrounding vineyards were leased to Rolayne and Ronald Stortz, who reside in a stately Victorian farmhouse downslope from the working part of the ranch.

The Stortzes make some of their Zinfandel from grapes whose vines were planted by the Picchettis around the turn of the century. Annual production is a modest twenty-five hundred cases.

Visitors to the winery and hikers enjoying the surrounding trails can park and walk a few hundred yards to the ranch buildings. Several shaded tables are set up on the grass around the winery.

THE WINE LIST
Pinot Blanc
Chardonnay
White Riesling
Pinot Noir
Zinfandel
Cabernet Sauvignon

VINTNER'S CHOICES
WHITE: *Pinot Blanc*
RED: *Pinot Noir*

SUNRISE WINERY
13100 MONTEBELLO ROAD
CUPERTINO, CA 95014
(408) 741-1310

HOURS: *11 a.m.– 3 p.m. Friday through Sunday*
TASTINGS: *Yes*
CHARGE FOR TASTING: *No*
TOURS: *No*
PICNIC AREA: *Yes*
RETAIL SALES: *Yes*

DIRECTIONS: *From Interstate 280, exit at Foothill Expressway and drive southwest (Foothill becomes Stevens Canyon Road) for approximately three miles to Montebello Road. Turn right and drive just over a half-mile to the ranch parking area on the left. From here it's a short stroll to the winery.*

RIDGE VINEYARDS

Cupertino

On a clear day, the skyscrapers of San Francisco's financial district are visible. Below, the high-technology capital of the world sprawls along the valley floor. As we drank the view with a glass of Ridge Zinfandel, the name Paradox Ridge seemed a more suitable moniker for this winery.

Even though computers have made their way into this internationally famous winemaking establishment, the rustic ranch scene that greets visitors at Ridge Vineyards stands in contrast to Silicon Valley below.

That's part of the tradition at Ridge, where the old ways apply to both aesthetics and winemaking. The winery actually exists in a couple of parts. The lower site — formerly the old Torre Winery — houses offices and case storage. Dr. Osea Perrone's 1885-era Monte Bello Winery, a three-level limestone structure, is the actual production facility and is not open to the public.

The winery's story picks up in 1949 when theologian William Short bought the Torre Winery and vineyard and replanted to Cabernet Sauvignon. Dave Bennion, a Stanford Research Institute (SRI) staffer,

arrived on the scene a decade later, when he crafted a whopping ten gallons of Cabernet. The families rebonded the winery in 1962, and five years later Dave left SRI to devote his full attentions to running the newly incorporated Ridge Winery. Shortly thereafter the Perrone property was purchased.

Acclaimed winemaker Paul Draper, whose name has become synonymous with Ridge (as well as California Zinfandel), joined the winery in 1969, after setting up a winery in the Chilean coastal mountains. Paul's style is one that eschews technology. He prefers, he says, to "intrude as little as possible on the natural process, drawing all the richness from the fruit into the wine."

A spacious tasting room was built in 1991. No less than six pairs of French doors frame the million-dollar view.

THE WINE LIST
Chardonnay
Petite Sirah
Zinfandel
Cabernet Sauvignon
Merlot

VINTNER'S CHOICES
WHITE: *Chardonnay*
   (Santa Cruz Mountains)
RED: *Zinfandel*

RIDGE VINEYARDS
17100 MONTEBELLO ROAD
P.O. BOX 1810
CUPERTINO, CA 95015
(408) 867-3244

HOURS: *Weekdays by appointment; 11 a.m.–3 p.m. Saturday and Sunday*
TASTINGS: *Yes*
CHARGE FOR TASTING: *No*
TOURS: *By appointment*
PICNIC AREA: *Yes*
RETAIL SALES: *Yes*

DIRECTIONS: *From Interstate 280, exit at Foothill Expressway and drive southwest (Foothill becomes Stevens Canyon Road) for approximately three miles to Montebello Road. Turn right and drive just over four miles up the winding road to winery.*

HALLCREST VINEYARDS AND THE ORGANIC WINE WORKS

Felton

*I*n establishing Hallcrest Vineyards in the early 1940s, San Francisco lawyer Chaffee Hall set out to produce European-quality wines on his own Santa Cruz mountains estate. Striving for excellence in a region not well known for fine wines, the maverick vintner spared no expense or effort, planting vines imported from Europe and enlisting help from a University of California professor.

True to his word, Hall turned his burgeoning winery into a leader. Although it garnered awards for Cabernet Sauvignon and Johannisberg Riesling at the California State Fair for more than a decade, Hallcrest enjoyed only fleeting fame. Hall died in 1964 and the winery closed for twelve years.

A small corporation operated the property as Felton-Empire Vineyards from 1976 until John Schumacher and his family took over and reclaimed the Hallcrest name just over a decade later. John first experimented with winemaking at the age of fourteen, while his parents were on vacation. By age

THE WINE LIST
Chardonnay
Sauvignon Blanc
White Riesling
Semillon
Cabernet Sauvignon
Barbera
Pinot Noir
Zinfandel
Merlot
Red table wine

VINTNER'S CHOICES
WHITE: *Estate White Riesling*
RED: *Clos de Jeannine,*
proprietary red table wine

**HALLCREST VINEYARDS
AND THE ORGANIC WINE
WORKS
379 FELTON EMPIRE ROAD
FELTON, CA 95018
(408) 335-4441; TOLL-FREE IN
CA: (800) 491-WINE**

HOURS: *11 a.m.–5:30 p.m.
daily*
TASTINGS: *Yes*
CHARGE FOR TASTING: *No*
TOURS: *By appointment*
PICNIC AREA: *Yes*
RETAIL SALES: *Yes*

DIRECTIONS: *From Highway
17, exit at Mt. Hermon Road
in Scotts Valley. Follow Mt.
Hermon Road to Graham Hill
Road, where a right turn leads
to Felton's main intersection.
Graham Hill Road becomes
Felton Empire Road. Winery
is on left.*

twenty-four, he and his wife, Lorraine, had converted their garage into a winery; in 1987 they moved the operation to the Felton site. John's sister, Shirin, joined as a partner.

A self-described nontraditional winemaker, John is an outspoken proponent of organically made wine. At the time of our visit, Hallcrest was marketing eight such wines — produced without the addition of sulfites — under the Organic Wine Works label.

The winery's tasting room, one of the most inviting in the Santa Cruz mountains, sits atop the working winery with a commanding vista of vineyards and hills. Hallcrest Vineyards hosts an annual Bluegrass Arts and Wine Festival in the spring.

BONNY DOON VINEYARD

Bonny Doon

If you call for directions to Bonny Doon Vineyard, the staff is likely to tell you that the tasting room is downtown Bonny Doon. They may add that it also functions as the aerodrome for the Flying Cigar. (It's a long story, and worth the trip to hear.)

When you get there you'll be entertained by the winery's now-famous whimsically creative labels like Big House Red, in which a spotlit rope of tied bed sheets hangs from a prison cell while a getaway car speeds away.

Suffice it to say that while the folks at Bonny Doon Vineyards are serious about making wine, they know how to have a good time.

Nary a parking space was available during my weekend visit to this popular winery, whose grounds are fringed with towering redwoods.

The tasting room, which in an earlier life was known as the Lost Weekend Saloon, sits next to Bonny Doon Road. The art-bedecked winery facilities are just upslope.

In addition to creating well-known varietals such as Gewurztraminer and Riesling, owner/vintner Randall Grahm grows rarely planted, sun-loving grapes such as Mourvedre, Roussane,

Marsanne, and Grenache. Juices from these fruits are made into wines bearing names like Le Sophiste, a Roussanne-Marsanne blend; and Vin Gris de Cigare, concocted from Grenache, Mourvedre, Cinsault, and Pinot Nero. Randall also crafts small batches of distilled spirits from fruits and grapes using an Alsatian still.

Bonny Doon Vineyard's wines are described in immensely (and somewhat cryptically) entertaining prose in a spec sheet published regularly by Randall. For example, he describes his 1991 Ca' del Solo Il Pescatore as the "Otis Redding cuvee," and the 1990 Old Telegram (Mourvedre) as a wine "absolutely loaded with blackberry, anise, and that earthy *je ne sais quoi* that moves Bandoliers to song."

About the 1991 Ca' del Solo Big House Red, he candidly wrote, "This wine is not for the faint of heart. It is quite black — black licorice, blackberry, black truffle, and earth. Enjoyable now for those who like to suffer."

Bonny Doon wines are so popular that sales of a few varieties are limited. During our visit, the winery's Santa Cruz Mountains Syrah carried a two-bottle limit.

THE WINE LIST
Gewurztraminer (Vin de Glaciere)
Vin Gris de Cigare, a dry, fruity
    pink wine
Malvasia Bianca
Chardonnay
Il Pescatore
Moscato del Solo
Riesling
Le Sophiste
Blanc de Noir (Pinot Meunier)
Le Cigare Volant
Mourvedre (Old Telegram)
Muscat Canelli (Vin de Glaciere)
Grenache (Clos de Gilroy)
Various distilled spirits

VINTNER'S CHOICES
WHITE: *Le Sophiste*
RED: *Le Cigare Volant*

BONNY DOON VINEYARD
10 PINE FLAT ROAD
BONNY DOON, CA
(408) 425-3625
MAILING ADDRESS:
P.O. BOX 8376
SANTA CRUZ, CA 95061

HOURS: *Summer: 12 p.m.–5 p.m.,*
closed Tuesday; winter:
12 p.m.–5 p.m., Thursday
through Monday
TASTINGS: *Yes*
CHARGE FOR TASTING: *No*
TOURS: *By appointment*
PICNIC AREA: *Yes*
RETAIL SALES: *Yes*

DIRECTIONS: *From Highway 1,*
one mile south of Davenport,
drive east on Bonny Doon Road
for 3.7 miles to fork in road (right
fork becomes Pine Flat Road).
Tasting room is on the right.

BARGETTO WINERY

Soquel

At Bargetto Winery in Soquel, winemaking is an almost exclusive family affair. Beverly, Martin, John, Richard, Loretta, and Tom all share the Bargetto name, and each lends his or her own special talent to the operation.

Bargetto has been a fixture in this Santa Cruz County hamlet since 1933, the year Prohibition ended. John and Philip Bargetto, sons of an Italian winemaker who immigrated in the late 1800s, chose the year of Repeal to convert their truck farm into a small winery. They began,

inauspiciously enough, making bulk wines for local retailers and restaurants.

John's son, Lawrence, guided the operation into its second generation and introduced fruit wines to the roster. The apricot, mead, plum, raspberry, and olallieberry wines are still some of Bargetto's most popular.

After Lawrence's death in 1982, his widow, Beverly, assumed the presidency of the company. Son Martin serves as general manager, with a cadre of dedicated siblings and cousins rounding out the list of Bargetto staff.

Using grapes from other California vineyards, the Bargetto family produces varietal wines and a sparkling wine in addition to the dessert wines.

Samples are poured within and outside a spacious and friendly tasting room and gift shop that sits on the bank of scenic Soquel Creek. Inside is a long dark bar set before a picture window facing the wooded creek. If the weather cooperates, the Bargettos open the only fully equipped, outdoor tasting bar we visited during our backroad winery travels. Bargetto operates another tasting room at 700 Cannery Row in Monterey.

THE WINE LIST
Sauvignon Blanc
Chardonnay
Dry Gewurztraminer
Sparkling Pinot Noir
White Zinfandel
Cabernet Sauvignon
Pinot Noir
Dessert and fruit wines

VINTNER'S CHOICES
WHITE: *Santa Cruz Mountain*
    Chardonnay
RED: *Santa Cruz Mountain*
    Cabernet Sauvignon

BARGETTO WINERY
3535 NORTH MAIN STREET
SANTA CRUZ, CA 95073
(408) 475-2258

HOURS: *9 a.m.–5 p.m.*
Monday through Saturday;
11 a.m.–5 p.m. Sunday
TASTINGS: *Yes*
CHARGE FOR TASTING: *No*
TOURS: *Yes*
PICNIC AREA: *Yes*
RETAIL SALES: *Yes*

DIRECTIONS: *From Highway 1 south of Santa Cruz, take the Capitola/Soquel exit and turn north away from the coast to Main Street. Make an immediate right turn on Main Street and follow for one mile through Soquel to winery on left.*

KIRIGIN CELLARS

Gilroy

Before visiting winemaster Nikola Kirigin-Chargin, we offer a few tips. Don't ask him to describe his wines. He won't. Don't ask him to list stores that sell them. There aren't any. Don't ask him about wine competitions. He disdains them. Finally, don't ask him about Eastern European politics. That is, unless you're prepared for a lively conversation.

California's back-country wine roads are full of maverick vintners, but of all those we encountered, Nikola Kirigin-Chargin is probably

the most outspokenly independent.

It was Nikola's strong set of personal convictions that led him from the Croatian Coast to Santa Clara's Uvas Valley. A 1941 graduate of the University of Zagreb's enology program, Nikola planned to follow the footsteps of several preceding generations by operating the family vineyard and winery. His career was interrupted when the communists took over (Croatia became Yugoslavia) and eventually confiscated the family's business. Although he lived under communist rule for more than a decade, Nikola decided to leave his homeland in 1959. "I could live without wine, but not without freedom," he said.

Nikola's American journey took him to both California and New York where he practiced the winemaker's craft. At about the time he planned to retire, an opportunity came along to purchase the historic Bonesio

THE WINE LIST

Sauvignon Blanc
Chardonnay
Sauvignon Vert
Gewurztraminer
Blanc de Noir
Malvasia Bianca
Pinot Noir
Cabernet Sauvignon
Zinfandel
Opol, a rosé blend popular along
*   the Croatian coast*
Vino deMocca dessert wine
Sparkling wine

KIRIGIN CELLARS
11550 WATSONVILLE ROAD
GILROY, CA 95020
(408) 847-8827

HOURS: *10 a.m.– 5 p.m. daily*
TASTINGS: *Yes*
CHARGE FOR TASTING: *No*
TOURS: *Yes*
PICNIC AREA: *Yes*
RETAIL SALES: *Yes*

DIRECTIONS: *From Highway 101, take the Tennant Avenue exit and drive west to Monterey Road. Turn left on Monterey Road and right on Watsonville Road. Follow Watsonville Road into the hills to winery on left, just past the Uvas Road intersection. From Hecker Pass Highway (Highway 152), drive north on Watsonville Road to winery on right.*

Winery, established in 1833. Nikola bought the winery in 1976 and changed the name to Kirigin (pronounced kuh-REE-gun) Cellars.

Now well into his seventies, the vintner continues to delight not only in making and drinking wine but in his role as a crusader against wine snobbery. Because he feels wine shouldn't be judged or described ("You either like it or you don't"), Nikola refuses to enter wine contests or pursue the opinions of wine critics ("Wine should have just one judge: the person drinking it"); sell his wine for more than $10 per bottle ("People should boycott expensive wine"); or to sell through wine distributors. His is sold only at the tasting room.

Visitors to Kirigin Cellars enter the unassuming, dimly lit tasting room through a door fashioned from a weathered wine barrel. The room sits behind the family residence, a grand old home once owned by a wealthy cattle baron.

SYCAMORE CREEK VINEYARDS

Morgan Hill

One of the central coast's most picturesque scenes greets visitors to Sycamore Creek Vineyards. Although it's a scene that has changed little in the winery's nearly hundred-year life, the property itself has enjoyed a varied succession of owners.

The Marchetti family started the operation in the early 1900s, building the winery and planting vines, some of which are still producing grapes.

Former schoolteachers Terry and Mary Kaye Parks bought the property in 1975, lovingly restoring the old buildings while planting new acreage. They also created an attractively rustic tasting area out of the hayloft inside the old winery. Large windows provide sweeping views of the creek, vineyards, and distant mountains.

The most recent change here occurred in 1989, when the Japanese sake-making Morita Company bought the property.

Picnic facilities are not available at Sycamore Creek Vineyards, but Santa Clara County maintains a small picnic and rest area just a few miles away on Watsonville Road, between the winery and Hecker Pass Highway (Highway 152).

THE WINE LIST
Chardonnay
Johannisberg Riesling
Sauvignon Blanc
Gamay Blanc
Carignane
Zinfandel
Cabernet Sauvignon

VINTNER'S CHOICES
WHITE: *Gamay Blanc*
RED: *Zinfandel*

**SYCAMORE CREEK
VINEYARDS
12775 UVAS ROAD
MORGAN HILL, CA 95037
(408) 779-4738**

HOURS: *11:30 a.m.–5 p.m. weekends*
TASTINGS: *Yes*
CHARGE FOR TASTING: *No*
TOURS: *By appointment*
PICNIC AREA: *No*
RETAIL SALES: *Yes*

DIRECTIONS: *From Highway 101, take the Tennant Avenue exit and drive west to Monterey Road. Turn left on Monterey Road and right on Watsonville Road. Follow Watsonville Road into the hills to Uvas Road and turn right. Winery is on left. From Hecker Pass Highway (Highway 152), drive north on Watsonville Road to Uvas Road and turn left to winery on left.*

FORTINO WINERY

Gilroy

A few months after Nikola Kirigin-Chargin of Kirigin Cellars (see separate entry) left his Eastern European homeland for America, a young fifth-generation winemaker named Ernest Fortino was making plans to move his family from Calabria in Southern Italy to the new world.

After working in other Northern California wineries, Ernest bought a "wonderful little vineyard" at the top of Hecker Pass in Gilroy in 1970. The family built what today is a thriving operation producing some thirty thousand cases of more than twenty wines, most of them sold here.

A gregarious man with expressive hands and an engaging smile, Ernest relies on winemaking traditions learned in Italy at a tender age. (He remembers stomping grapes at age six.) Although he later studied winemaking in France, Ernest says "making wine is a natural process.

It has less to do with chemistry and books. Our laboratory doesn't tell me how to make my wine."

In addition to Ernest, who steers the helm of the business, Fortino Winery is staffed by wife Marie, winemaking son Gino, daughter Teri, and son-in-law Brian.

Among the many wines produced here are Charbono, a full-bodied red that hails from the Italian-French border region, and Malavasia Bianca, a slightly sweet white wine made from grapes that were grown originally in Sicily. The Fortinos' vineyards are not irrigated, which tends to produce grapes with greater sugar content. For fermentation, Ernest favors wood over steel and cement.

The Fortino operation consists of the winery, ample storage areas, bottling facilities, an office, a large tasting room and gift shop, and an Italian deli stocked with delicious breads, cheeses, and meats. Visitors may create a custom picnic and walk across the parking lot to a series of tables next to the vineyards.

THE WINE LIST
Chardonnay
Chablis
Sauvignon Blanc
White Zinfandel
Johannisberg Riesling
Chenin Blanc
Malvasia Bianca
Pinot Noir
Burgundy Reserve
Zinfandel
Petit Sirah
Charbono
Sparkling wine

VINTNER'S CHOICES
WHITE: *Chardonnay*
RED: *Charbono*

FORTINO WINERY
4525 HECKER PASS HIGHWAY
GILROY, CA 95020
(408) 842-3305

HOURS: *9 a.m.–5 p.m. daily*
TASTINGS: *Yes*
CHARGE FOR TASTING: *No*
TOURS: *Yes*
PICNIC AREA: *Yes*
RETAIL SALES: *Yes*

DIRECTIONS: *From Monterey Road in Gilroy (runs parallel to Highway 101), drive west on First Street, which becomes Hecker Pass Highway (Highway 152). Drive to top of pass to winery on right.*

LIVE OAKS WINERY

Gilroy

*W*ith a tasting room displaying hanging Christmas ornaments year round, what might be the largest display of celebrity photos in the United States, and other unconventional bric-a-brac, Live Oaks wins the award for the most unusual of our backroad coastal mountain wineries.

This venerable winery was started in 1912 by Italian emigrant Eduardo Scagliotti, whose son, Peter, later brought the infusion of whimsy to the tasting room. Peter died in 1988, shortly after selling the operation to Richard Blocher, who runs the adjacent Western Tree Nursery. Mitsuo

Takemoto has served as winemaker at Live Oaks for several years.

Although there are other buildings on the property, only the tasting room, which sits at the end of the lane, is open to the public. Most visitors, however, will be more than entertained browsing among the curios that fill the tasting room and lingering at tables in an adjacent outdoor picnic area.

In addition to its roster of mostly white wines, Live Oaks markets red and white wine vinegar.

THE WINE LIST
Chenin Blanc
Chardonnay
Gewurztraminer
Johannisberg Riesling
Sauvignon Blanc
Haut Sauterne
White Zinfandel
Zinfandel
Burgundy

VINTNER'S CHOICES
WHITE: *Chardonnay*
RED: *Premium Burgundy*

LIVE OAKS WINERY
3875 HECKER PASS HIGHWAY
GILROY, CA 95020
(408) 842-2401

HOURS: *10 a.m.–5 p.m. daily;*
closed major holidays
TASTINGS: *Yes*
CHARGE FOR TASTING: *No*
TOURS: *No*
PICNIC AREA: *Yes*
RETAIL SALES: *Yes*

DIRECTIONS: *From Monterey*
Road in Gilroy (runs parallel to
Highway 101), drive west on
First Street, which becomes
Hecker Pass Highway (Highway
152). Drive four and one-half
miles to winery on right.

The Sierra Foothills

To Sacramento
Placerville
▼ BOEGER WINERY
Carson Rd.
To South Lake Tahoe
50
49
E16
PERRY CREEK
▼ VINEYARDS
Steiner Rd.
Fairplay Rd.
STORY
▼ VINEYARDS
FITZPATRICK
WINERY
▼ KARLY
WINES
SHENANDOAH
VINEYARDS
▼
Mt. Akum
Omo Ranch Rd.
E16
▼ SOBON ESTATE
▼ LATCHAM VINEYARDS
Plymouth
▼ MONTEVIÑA
WINES
49
STEVENOT
WINERY ▼
Murphys
BLACK SHEEP
VINEYARDS ▼
MILLIAIRE
WINERY ▼
Main Street
To Angels Camp
Murhphys
Grade
Road
Six-Mile Rd.
4
▼ CHATOM
VINEYARDS
KAUTZ ▼
VINEYARDS
To Angels
Camp

MONTEVIÑA WINERY

Plymouth

*L*ouis "Bob" Trinchero was a twelve-year-old New Yorker in 1947 when his father Mario and his uncle John bought Napa Valley's now-famous Sutter Home Winery and moved their families out West. Bob learned the wine business from the ground up, starting out shoveling pomace and washing barrels.

By his mid-twenties, Bob had become Sutter Home's winemaker and worked to upgrade the product line by improving varietal quality and phasing out many jug wines.

The Sutter Home connection with the foothills was made in 1968, when Bob tasted an impressive homemade Zinfandel from century-old Amador County vines. He quickly located the source — the Deaver Ranch outside Plymouth — and began bottling Sutter Home Amador County Zinfandel.

Twenty years later Bob solidified his ties with Amador County by purchasing Monteviña Winery.

Established in 1970, Monteviña had earned a reputation primarily for its robust Zinfandels and Barberas. Bob fully intends to build on that tradition. In 1990, Monteviña planted fifty new acres of vines devoted to classic Italian varietals. In addition to Zinfandel, these include Sangiovese, the principal variety in the Chianti district; Nebbiolo, used to make Barolo and Barbaresco wines; Barbera, from the Piedmonte region; Refosco, found mostly in Northern Italy; and Aleatico, from Southern Italy.

Bob's purchase of another nearby sixty-three-acre vineyard comprised mostly of Barbera is expected to make Monteviña the nation's largest grower and producer of premium Barbera.

The Trincheros have also established an experimental vineyard in the Sacramento Delta region in an effort to evaluate some fifty other Italian grape varieties, some of which are no longer grown in Italy. The family plans to identify the most promising for commercial cultivation.

The winery's modern facilities are a popular destination for wine tourists. The tasting room is spacious and friendly, and the large, trellis-covered picnic area adjacent to the vineyards is one of the region's most inviting.

THE WINE LIST
Chardonnay
White Zinfandel
Fumé Blanc
Zinfandel
Reserve Zinfandel
Barbera
Montanaro, a Zinfandel and
   Barbera blend
Brioso, a lighter Zinfandel
Cabernet Sauvignon

VINTNER'S CHOICES
WHITE: *Fume Blanc*
RED: *Zinfandel Reserve*

MONTEVIÑA WINERY
20680 SHENANDOAH
SCHOOL ROAD
PLYMOUTH, CA 95669
(209) 245-6942

HOURS: *11 a.m.–4 p.m. daily*
TASTINGS: *Yes*
CHARGE FOR TASTING: *No*
TOURS: *No*
PICNIC AREA: *Yes*
RETAIL SALES: *Yes*

DIRECTIONS: *From Highway 49, drive east on Shenandoah Road (Highway E16) for two-and-a-half miles. Turn right on Shenandoah School Road and drive two miles to the winery on the right.*

SHENANDOAH VINEYARDS

Plymouth

*S*henandoah Vineyards has come a long way since the days when a first-year commercial vintner named Leon Sobon virtually lived in a wine-laden station wagon. For the better part of that year, he drove from store to store and restaurant to restaurant selling his first fourteen hundred cases. That was in 1977.

More than fifteen years later, Shenandoah Vineyards is producing some forty-five thousand cases each year and is now one of the Mother Lode's largest wineries. During bottling time, the Sobons fill as many cases in one day as they did during their entire first year.

When Leon retired from his career in Palo Alto as a Lockheed ceramic engineer in 1977, he and his wife, Shirley, were understandably

wary of their ability to support six growing children with a brand-new winery, using skills learned as amateur home winemakers. As it turned out, the kids grew to play a major role in the winery's success.

Shenandoah Vineyards and the clan's newest operation, Sobon Estate (see following entry), epitomize family business. Son Paul serves as co-winemaker and handles out-of-state marketing duties, son Robert is the resident computer expert and handles promotion, son Kenneth works at the winery during the summers, daughter Carol assists with Bay Area marketing, and Carol's husband, Tom, is Northern California sales manager. Shirley has overall responsibility for the finances and Leon supervises the one hundred acres of vineyards and makes the wine.

Leon and Shirley both agreed early on to create distinctive labels for their wines, and since 1979 they have incorporated original art in their label designs. It should come as no surprise, then, that the Shenandoah

Vineyards tasting room doubles as an art gallery, with changing exhibitions by Northern California sculptors and artists.

Only slightly more than 10 percent of Shenandoah Vineyards' wines are sold through the Sobons' backroad winery tasting room. Most are sold in California stores and restaurants, although the family is seeing out-of-state demand grow.

Though in recent years Leon and Shirley Sobon have come to rely on others to distribute their wines throughout the United States, they haven't forgotten their roots. For six weeks each year the couple sets aside time to make personal calls on major accounts. Nowadays, however, they leave the station wagon and wine at home.

THE WINE LIST
Sauvignon Blanc
White Zinfandel
Zinfandel
Cabernet Sauvignon
Port
Orange Muscat
Black Muscat

VINTNER'S CHOICES
WHITE: *Sauvignon Blanc*
RED: *Zinfandel Special Reserve*

SHENANDOAH VINEYARDS
12300 STEINER ROAD
PLYMOUTH, CA 95669
(209) 245-4455

HOURS: *10 a.m.–5 p.m. daily*
TASTINGS: *Yes*
CHARGE FOR TASTING: *No*
TOURS: *By appointment*
PICNIC AREA: *Yes*
RETAIL SALES: *Yes*

DIRECTIONS: *From Highway 49 at Plymouth, drive east from Highway 49 onto Shenandoah Road (Highway E16) and turn left on Steiner Road to winery lane on right.*

SOBON ESTATE

Plymouth

Ĵohn Sutter wasn't the only Swiss emigrant who played a role in shaping California history. True, the name of fellow countryman Adam Uhlinger isn't as famous as Sutter's, but the Uhlinger winery outlived Sutter's Coloma mill and his Sacramento fort. (The current structures bearing those names are largely reconstructions.) The venerable Plymouth winery started by Uhlinger in 1856 is the third oldest winemaking operation in California and quite possibly the site of the Golden State's first plantings of Zinfandel grapes.

This classic home and winery is a veritable wine shrine. The cellar is virtually unchanged since the gold rush days, when miners would sample vintages from the tasting barrels and fill their jugs with the wines of their choice. The old oval casks, constructed of local white oak, were handcrafted with deeply concave fronts — the style preferred by Germanic coopers of yesterday. Atop the cellar sits the Uhlinger homestead, a modest white house backed by vineyards.

The Uhlingers ultimately sold the winery to the D'Agostini family, whose members made wine here for well over a half-century. The winery even continued operations during Prohibition by making sacramental wines. Leon and Shirley Sobon, who developed the nearby Shenandoah Vineyards (see previous listing), bought the property in 1989 and changed its name to Sobon Estate.

While the Sobons were primarily motivated by the prospects of expanding their vineyard holdings, they have gone to great lengths to preserve the rich history of the estate. The dark stone cellar and adjacent buildings are known today as the Shenandoah Valley Museum.

After a taste or two in a separate building, visitors are encouraged to take a self-guided tour of the growing museum. First stop is the fermenting tank and display room. The hundreds of intriguing artifacts on display here trace the viticultural and agricultural history of the Shenandoah Valley. The items range from coopers' tools to wagons.

From here, you'll stroll into the storage area, among towering redwood tanks that boasted a combined 150,000 gallon capacity. In the adjacent cellar, made of locally quarried stone and oak timbers, the winery's original casks still stand side by side.

Unfortunately, the years haven't been so kind to the vineyards, where phylloxera have destroyed all of the original Zinfandel vines. The vineyard currently consists of some sixty-five acres of Zinfandel, about a dozen acres of Sauvignon Blanc, and seven acres of Cabernet Sauvignon.

Among Sobon Estate's more intriguing products is Muscat Canelli, a sweet, smooth, accessible white dessert wine.

THE WINE LIST
Fume Blanc
Zinfandel
Cabernet Sauvignon
Cabernet Franc
Syrah
Muscat Canelli

VINTNER'S CHOICES
WHITE: *Sobon Estate*
   Fume Blanc
RED: *Sobon Estate*
   Zinfandel

SOBON ESTATE
14430 SHENANDOAH
ROAD
PLYMOUTH, CA 95669
(209) 245-6554

HOURS: *10 a.m.–5 p.m. daily*
TASTINGS: *Yes*
CHARGE FOR TASTING: *No*
TOURS: *Self-guided museum tours*
PICNIC AREA: *Yes*
RETAIL SALES: *Yes*

DIRECTIONS: *From Highway 49 at Plymouth, drive seven miles east on Shenandoah Road (Highway E16) to winery on right. Sobon Estate is approximately forty-five miles from Sacramento.*

KARLY WINES

Plymouth

Our award for the most remote backroad foothill winery goes to Buck and Karly Cobb, who live and work at the end of a winding, half-mile gravel road outside Plymouth. When we visited Karly winery, getting there turned out to be half the fun. We stopped at least a couple of times along the driveway to photograph finely sculpted oaks, a weathered barn, and an old wine cask-turned-directional sign.

When the Cobbs moved here in 1976, constructing a winery wasn't even remotely part of the plan. Buck, a former Air Force fighter pilot

who saw action during the Korean War, had logged seventeen years as a research engineer at high-profile California think tanks like the Stanford Research Institute.

Looking for something new, he accepted a job forecasting energy needs for utilities with the California Energy Commission and moved with Karly from the Bay Area to sleepy Amador County. Early retirement on their sprawling 110-acre ranch would have been the next step, had it not been for the influence of nearby wineries like Shenandoah and Monteviña.

As it is wont to do, the winemaking bug worked slowly at first. Buck initially took it up as a hobby, but before long he was planting vines and ordering winemaking equipment. Soon he exchanged his office job for a fourth career as a commercial vintner.

Assisted by only one other full-time staffer, Buck and Karly have kept the operation relatively small since opening the winery in 1980. The vineyard is twenty acres and annual production is only about ten thousand cases. Except for their Chardonnay, made from grapes grown in the Edna Valley near San Luis Obispo, the Karlys use either their own grapes or fruit from other Amador County vineyards.

Buck employs a special process of fermenting his red wines that results in what he describes as a fruitier flavor with less tannin. "Our wines are probably the most robust in the county," he noted.

THE WINE LIST
Sauvignon Blanc
Chardonnay
White Zinfandel
Zinfandel
Petite Sirah (sold only at winery)
Syrah

VINTNER'S CHOICES
WHITE: *Sauvignon Blanc*
RED: *Zinfandel*

KARLY WINES
11076 BELL ROAD
PLYMOUTH, CA 95669
(209) 245-3922

HOURS: *12 p.m.– 4 p.m. daily*
TASTINGS: *Yes*
CHARGE FOR TASTING: *No*
TOURS: *By appointment*
PICNIC AREA: *Yes*
RETAIL SALES: *Yes*

DIRECTIONS: *From Highway 49 at Plymouth, drive east for four miles on Shenandoah Road (Highway E16). Turn left on Bell Road and drive one-half mile to winery drive on left. Follow gravel road one-half mile to winery.*

STORY VINEYARD

Plymouth

*I*n contrast to many backroad wineries that attempt to satisfy a range of consumer preferences by producing a little bit of this and a little bit of that, the Story family places most of its eggs, er, grapes into one basket — or, rather, barrel. This small family winery focuses its attention primarily on Zinfandel, the wine for which California's foothills have historically been known.

Eugene Story established the business in the early 1970s as Cosumnes River Vineyard, but he found over time that few of his customers outside the region could pronounce or remember the name.

Story assigned the family name to the winery in 1979.

Don't let the sight of Story's rather nondescript winery building on Bell Road dissuade you from a visit. This is one of the most pleasant diversions along the foothill wine road. Visitors are welcomed not at the winery proper but at a tiny, rustic tasting room that overlooks miles of rugged oak-studded terrain.

The lovely setting can best be savored from either the couple of tables on the tasting-room deck or from other tables set among the trees right at the edge of the canyon. In our opinion, this is the best backroad winery picnic spot in the region.

THE WINE LIST
Zinfandel
White Zinfandel
Chenin Blanc
Mission del Sol dessert wine

STORY VINEYARD
10525 BELL ROAD
PLYMOUTH, CA 95669
(209) 245-6208

HOURS: *By appointment weekdays; 11 a.m.–5 p.m. Saturday and Sunday*
TASTINGS: *Yes*
CHARGE FOR TASTING: *No*
TOURS: *Yes, informal*
PICNIC AREA: *Yes*
RETAIL SALES: *Yes*

DIRECTIONS: *From Highway 49 in Plymouth, drive east for four miles on Shenandoah Road (Highway E16). Turn left on Bell Road and follow for two miles to winery on right.*

In addition to several reasonably priced vintages of Zinfandel (ten-year-old Zins were still available during our visit), the Story family markets White Zinfandel and a small amount of Chenin Blanc. The winery also maintains one of the north state's last plots of old Mission vines, from which the Story family makes a sweet red dessert wine called Mission del Sol.

FITZPATRICK WINERY

Somerset

The hills outside of Somerset were a sun-dried golden brown as we made our way along a wide dirt road to the winemaking operation run by the Fitzpatrick clan. It's a most unlikely setting for the north state's only Irish winery.

This remote-but-popular enclave, thankfully inaccessible to tour buses, is operated by Brian and Diana Fitzpatrick, who have been making wine in this location since 1980. Among their best-known products is Eire Ban Sauvignon Blanc, made from organically grown

grapes. (Brian is a member of the California Certified Organic Farmers.)

A spacious tasting room occupies one end of a handsome lodge made of fir logs. After sampling the Fitzpatrick wares, visitors usually saunter out to a picnic table on a large deck that commands an awesome gold country vista.

For those who want to linger a bit longer, Brian and Diana offer five bed-and-breakfast guest rooms in the lodge. For many weary wine tourists, retiring to a room at the Fitzpatricks' lodge is the perfect way to end the day.

The winery is gaining a following for its multicultural dinner and musical celebrations held during the year.

The continually evolving series of feasts may range from Moroccan Madness to Alice in Curryland. Fitzpatrick also hosts an annual grape stomp in early fall.

The best way to learn about upcoming Fitzpatrick events is through an informative and entertaining newsletter sent free on request.

THE WINE LIST
Cabernet Sauvignon
  (estate bottled)
Chenin Blanc
Merlot
Zinfandel
Chardonnay
Sauvignon Blanc
Celtic cider

VINTNER'S CHOICES
WHITE: *Eire Ban Sauvignon*
  Blanc
RED: *Cabernet Sauvignon*

FITZPATRICK WINERY
7740 FAIRPLAY ROAD
SOMERSET, CA 95684
(209) 245-3248

HOURS: *11 a.m.–5 p.m. weekends, by appointment weekdays.*
TASTINGS: *Yes*
CHARGE FOR TASTING: *No*
TOURS: *No*
PICNIC AREA: *Yes*
RETAIL SALES: *Yes*

DIRECTIONS: *From Southbound Highway E16 south of Somerset, turn left on Fairplay Road and follow to the Fitzpatrick sign on right. Follow dirt road to winery. The community of Somerset is also referred to as Fairplay.*

LATCHAM VINEYARDS

Mt. Aukum

Latcham Vineyards may be a relatively young label, but Franklin and Patty Latcham's involvement in the Sierra foothills wine industry has been brewing since 1980. That's when the Bay Area couple realized a longtime dream by starting their own vineyard.

Franklin, an internationally known tax attorney who has since stepped away from a full-time law practice (he still consults from time to time), bought a portion of an old horse and cattle ranch outside Mt. Aukum and started growing grapes on virgin soil.

Once their vineyards began to flourish, Franklin and Patty entered into an agreement with nearby Granite Springs Winery, where Latcham wines have been made since 1990. The final big step in the Latcham

Vineyards evolution involved expanding the existing facilities to create an estate winery. Construction was just getting under way at the time of our visit.

The lane into the family's forty-acre ranch brings visitors to the edge of the vineyards and a small, tree-shaded barn that serves as both tasting room and storage facility. The home of Franklin and Patty stands nearby, overlooking the vineyard and a large pond. Also living on the property are son Jonathan and daughter-in-law Joyce. Jonathan manages the twenty-six acres of Latcham vines and Joyce oversees the office.

While nearby Shenandoah Valley vintners have difficulty growing temperature-sensitive Chardonnay grapes because of the intense summer heat, the Latchams' rolling property creeps well above the 2,000 foot level. Their Chardonnay plot, which sits at about 2,300 feet, has thrived.

The Latchams are also proud of their Special Reserve Estate Zinfandel, produced from vines that originally were cut from seventy-year-old Sonoma County Zinfandel vines. Franklin describes the wine as "rich and complex, almost Cabernet-like."

THE WINE LIST
Chardonnay
Sauvignon Blanc
White Zinfandel
Chenin Blanc
El Dorado White table wine
El Dorado Red table wine
Cabernet Sauvignon
Zinfandel
Petite Sirah

VINTNER'S CHOICES
WHITE: *Chardonnay*
RED: *Zinfandel*

LATCHAM VINEYARDS
2860 OMO RANCH ROAD
P.O. BOX 80
MT. AUKUM, CA 95656
(209) 245-6834 OR
(209) 245-6642

HOURS: *11 a.m.–5 p.m.*
Wednesday through Sunday;
closed Monday and Tuesday
TASTINGS: *Yes*
CHARGE FOR TASTING: *No*
TOURS: *Yes*
PICNIC AREA: *Yes*
RETAIL SALES: *Yes*

DIRECTIONS: *From Highway 49 at Plymouth, drive east on Shenandoah Road (Highway E16) for ten miles to Mt. Aukum. At the Mt. Aukum/Omo Ranch Road Y, veer right onto Omo Ranch Road and drive one mile to winery lane on right.*

PERRY CREEK VINEYARDS

Somerset

*U*nlike the prosperous few who strike it rich and move to *Beverly Hills, sweater manufacturing magnate Mike Chazen traded a luxury lifestyle in the hills of Beverly for the rustic hills of the Mother Lode, swapping sweaters for Sauvignon.*

Before coming to the foothills to start Perry Creek Vineyards, Mike was an active partner in a thriving business that supplied sweaters to major clothing labels. "If you have sweaters at home, chances are at least one of them came from our company," he told us.

Since the factory happened to be in Korea, Mike spent about half his

time there. After a particularly grueling trip overseas, Mike decided to unwind with a leisurely drive from Southern California to the Reno rodeo. The trip took him and his wife, Alice, through the gold country where, as a lark, they pulled off the highway to look at property. About a year later he was a winemaker.

Although the 155-acre property near Somerset came with a mature Chenin Blanc vineyard, there was no paved road, no winery, and no label. Alice and Mike chose a secluded,

wooded spot and built not only a handsome Mission-style winery but a 5,000-square-foot home and a large warehouse to accommodate his other passion: buying, selling, and restoring vintage vehicles.

The vineyard has been expanded to include plantings of several other grape varieties, including Viognier, Nebbiolo, Sangiovese, and Cabernet Sauvignon.

In addition to housing winemaking equipment, the large winery building holds a changing display of vintage autos — all museum quality. The vehicles on view here represent only a small portion of Mike's collection, and he alternates them regularly to the delight of visitors.

THE WINE LIST
Cabernet Sauvignon
Dry Chenin Blanc
White Zinfandel
Zinfandel Nouveau
Sauvignon Blanc

VINTNER'S CHOICES
WHITE: *Dry Chenin Blanc*
RED: *Zinfandel Nouveau*

PERRY CREEK VINEYARDS
7400 PERRY CREEK ROAD
SOMERSET, CA 95684
(209) 245-5175

HOURS: *11 a.m.–5 p.m. Saturday and Sunday*
TASTINGS: *Yes*
CHARGE FOR TASTING: *No*
TOURS: *Self-guided*
PICNIC AREA: *Yes*
RETAIL SALES: *Yes*

DIRECTIONS: *From southbound Highway E16, turn left on Fairplay Road (south of Somerset) and make an immediate left on Perry Creek Road. Drive two and one-half miles to winery. The community of Somerset is also referred to as Fairplay.*

BOEGER WINERY

Placerville

One of California's oldest remaining winemaking establishments, the Lombardo Winery (now Boeger Winery) was actually a relative late-comer to the foothills when it opened in 1872. The first wineries sprang up in this region shortly after James Marshall touched off the gold rush in nearby Coloma in 1849. The Lombardo facility was among those that appeared on the scene to keep pace with the seemingly insatiable thirst of the hard-working and hard-playing miners.

After the gold gave out, however, the once-thriving local wine business nearly collapsed. It wasn't until the 1960s and 1970s that

folks like Greg and Susan Boeger began to rediscover the region's potential for growing wine grapes, especially Zinfandel. Susan and Greg were major players in the foothill wine renaissance.

Over the years, the Boegers have increased their acreage and built a brand-new winery on the property. Still, the most prominent landmark is the old winery building, which serves as the tasting room. The diminutive stone and mortar cellar, topped by a tin roof, is maintained in what can best be described as a state of arrested decay.

Still visible inside are the ceiling chutes through which the crushed grapes were once fed from what originally was the production area on the second floor.

The old Lombardo press is displayed along with other winery memorabilia assembled by the Boegers.

Adjacent to the tasting room and an aging barn is a lush picnic area with secluded tables shaded by old fig and apple trees. There's also a small pond here.

In addition to preserving the historic winery and grounds, Greg and Susan haven't lost touch with the rough-and-tumble past of Placerville, originally known as Hangtown. Two of the more popular Boeger wines carry the names Hangtown Red and Hangtown Gold.

Greg Boeger is a member of the Nichelini family, which has operated Nichelini Winery above St. Helena (see separate listing) for generations. Greg also serves as winemaker at Nichelini, and Boeger Winery provides grapes for some Nichelini wines.

THE WINE LIST
Zinfandel
Barbera
Meritage
Cabernet Sauvignon
Hangtown Red
Merlot
Sauvignon Blanc
Chardonnay
White Zinfandel
Johannisberg Riesling
Hangtown Gold

VINTNER'S CHOICES
WHITE: *Chardonnay*
RED: *Zinfandel*

BOEGER WINERY
1709 CARSON ROAD
PLACERVILLE, CA 95667
(916) 622-8094

HOURS: *10 a.m.–5 p.m. daily; closed holidays*
TASTINGS: *Yes*
CHARGE FOR TASTING: *No*
TOURS: *Informal*
PICNIC AREA: *Yes*
RETAIL SALES: *Yes*

DIRECTIONS: *From Highway 50 east of Placerville, exit north at Schnell School Road. At Carson Road, turn right to winery drive on left.*

CHATOM VINEYARDS

Douglas Flat

At many of the backroad wineries we've visited, learning about the past lives of the owners can be as interesting as learning about the wine. Such is the story of Gay Callan, proprietor of Chatom Vineyards and one of the most unlikely winery owners you'll meet in Northern California.

Descended from Mark Hopkins, one of the Big Four, who helped establish the transcontinental railroad, Gay was bred in the tony trappings of San Francisco. She attended exclusive schools and ultimately went on to earn an MBA degree. A successful career in broadcast marketing in San Francisco preceded her escape to the quieter life of Calaveras County in 1980.

During her first few years in the Mother Lode, Gay nursed a sixty-five-acre vineyard in Esmeralda Valley near San Andreas. Then, in 1985 she began producing limited edition, custom-crushed wines. Her charming L-shaped winery and tasting room, built of rammed earth and wood, opened in 1991.

In contrast to some of the rustic wineries nearby, Chatom hosts visitors in a spacious, modern tasting room with a gleaming tile floor and a beautiful oak bar. A number of gift and gourmet items are for sale along with Chatom wines. Production equipment and aging barrels are housed in the adjacent wing.

THE WINE LIST
Semillon
Calaveras Fume
Chardonnay
Zinfandel
Cabernet Sauvignon
Merlot

VINTNER'S CHOICES
WHITE: *Calaveras Fume*
RED: *Cabernet Sauvignon*

CHATOM VINEYARDS
1969 HIGHWAY 4
P.O. BOX 2730
DOUGLAS FLAT, CA 95229
(209) 736-6500

HOURS: *11 a.m.–4:30 p.m. daily*
TASTINGS: *Yes*
CHARGE FOR TASTING: No
TOURS: *By appointment*
PICNIC AREA: *Yes*
RETAIL SALES: *Yes*

DIRECTIONS: *The winery is two miles south of Murphys on Highway 4.*

MILLIAIRE WINERY

Murphys

*W*e've visited wineries housed in old barns, a foundry, a few caves, and even in an old hop kiln. But never had we seen one in a service station until our visit to Steve and Liz Millier's small wine-making operation in historic Murphys. A request to fill-'er-up here will get you a case or two of Cabernet Sauvignon, rather than a tank of gas.

The best known of Calaveras County's winemakers, Steve apprenticed in 1975 at David Bruce Winery in the Santa Cruz mountains before heading east to the Mother Lode. During the 1980s, he served as

winemaker at Murphys' Stevenot Winery and in 1989 was named vintner at the new Kautz Vineyards and Winery.

In the meantime, Steve and Liz started their own label, setting up shop in 1983 in an old carriage house-turned-filling station and garage. Murphys Creek, which flows just behind the building, provides natural cooling year round. Century-old buildings, including the venerable Murphys Hotel, are among the Milliers' neighbors.

Since Steve was making wine for several growers at the time, a Millier label might have caused some confusion. So the couple looked up the family name in a French dictionary and came up with Milliaire.

Visitors taste in the winery's no-frills office area. The big double-door garage where mechanics once toiled and carriages rested is now chockablock with aging barrelsful of wine. About one thousand cases are produced each year, all from grapes grown in the California foothills. (The Milliers own no vineyards.)

The first wine bottled each year is a Beaujolais-style White Zinfandel called Christmas Cuvee, offered on a limited basis during the holiday season.

While Milliaire Winery sits fairly inconspicuously along Main Street, the place buzzes during what Liz describes as the "fall road show." In the fall, the Milliers set up their crusher/stemmer and small basket press in front of the winery and put on a traffic-stopping harvest show that attracts considerable attention from Main Street passersby and from the friendly horses that live in the field across the street.

THE WINE LIST
Sauvignon Blanc
Chardonnay
Dry Gewurztraminer
Merlot
Cabernet Sauvignon
Zinfandel
Orange Muscat
Late Harvest Sauvignon Blanc
Late Harvest dessert-style
  Zinfandel

VINTNER'S CHOICES
WHITE: *Chardonnay*
RED: *Zinfandel (from old*
  foothill vines)

MILLIAIRE WINERY
276 MAIN STREET
P.O. BOX 1554
MURPHYS, CA 95247
(209) 728-1658

HOURS: *Daily*
TASTINGS: *11 a.m.–4:30 p.m.*
CHARGE FOR TASTING: *No*
TOURS: *Informal*
PICNIC AREA: *No*
RETAIL SALES: *Yes*

DIRECTIONS: *From eastbound Highway 4 in Murphys, turn left on Main Street to winery on right.*

BLACK SHEEP VINTNERS

Murphys

*I*n creating the original watercolor that would become the label for David and Janis Olson's wines, Mother Lode artist Annette Hart painted a shepherd guiding a flock of sheep. Among the flock is a lone black sheep, symbolizing the Olsons' desire to be different.

The desire to distinguish their fledgling winery sends Dave Olson on premium grape hunts every year. Because climate and soil conditions play such a critical role in determining the characteristics of a particular vintage, Dave says his wine style is chosen in the vineyard. "We basically only guide the wine while it's here (in the winery)." The annual search for the perfect grape takes him to vineyards up and down the foothills, where he selects small lots.

The Olsons crush in an old 1920s-era barn that had been converted to Chispa Cellars in the 1970s by pioneer Calaveras County winemaker Bob Bliss. The winery was the first in the county to be bonded. Dave and Jan bought the operation in the mid-1980s and changed the name to Black Sheep Vintners.

The weathered structure houses several dozen French and American oak barrels, as well as the tasting room. Dave and Jan's original small press sits out front, a reminder of the days when winemaking was an Olson family hobby.

In addition to their Black Sheep label, the Olsons bottle a wine or two each year under the whimsical True Frogs label, in celebration of the famous frog jump held each year just down the road in Angels Camp. Past True Frogs vintages have included Semillon, Symphony, and a table wine called Lily Pad White.

When asked what type of meal might best complement a Black Sheep Zinfandel, Dave and Jan offer an obvious choice: leg of lamb. And what goes well with Lily Pad White? We were afraid to ask.

THE WINE LIST
Zinfandel
Cabernet Sauvignon
Sauvignon Blanc
True Frogs Lily Pad White

VINTNER'S CHOICES
WHITE: *True Frogs Lily Pad White*
RED: *Zinfandel*

BLACK SHEEP VINTNERS
634 FRENCH GULCH ROAD
P.O. BOX 1851
MURPHYS, CA 95247
(209) 728-2157

HOURS: *12 p.m.–5 p.m. Saturday and Sunday or by appointment*
TASTINGS: *Yes*
CHARGE FOR TASTING: *No*
TOURS: *Informal*
PICNIC AREA: *No*
RETAIL SALES: *Yes*

DIRECTIONS: *The winery is located at the west end of Main Street at the intersection of Murphys Grade Road and French Gulch Road.*

KAUTZ VINEYARDS AND WINERY

Murphys

It wasn't until Lodi farm magnate John Kautz had made his mark with wheat, sugar beets, tomatoes, and bell peppers that he decided to try his hand at premium wine grapes. Selling exclusively to other wineries, it was ten years before he crafted his first wine. It took another decade to create a winery.

For wine-road tourists, however, this is one operation that was worth waiting for. The Kautz family's sprawling winery is without a doubt the Sierra foothills' most impressive.

From some sixty acres, John chose as the site for his winery the base of a small hill. He then proceeded to blast six hundred feet of tunnels out of solid rock, spraying the cavern walls with concrete. These expansive passageways, dimly lit by thousands of tiny lights, are lined with barrels of aging wines. Cascading water from a spring-fed fountain echoes throughout the caverns, enhancing the underground experience.

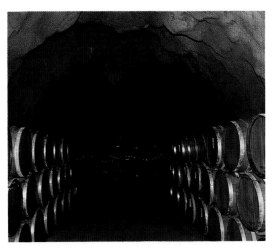

A small amphitheater provides an unusually harmonic setting for occasional musical events.

On my visit, the finishing touches were being placed on a grand tasting room that hovers over a large patio connecting the cave hill with a large cinder-block tank facility.

Kautz's goal is to build production to around twenty-five thousand cases annually. Wines are bottled as Ironstone Vineyards, the name given to the rolling acreage that surrounds the winery. Well-known foothill vintner Steve Millier (see Milliaire Winery listing) is the winemaker.

Visitors are invited to stroll the expansive grounds, which also boast a pond and oak-shaded picnic area. If your time in the foothills is limited, the Kautz operation is a must-see.

THE WINE LIST
Chardonnay
Triune, a Bordeaux-style
*   blend of Cabernet*
*   Sauvignon and Cabernet*
*   Franc*
Symphony
Merlot

VINTNER'S CHOICES
WHITE: *Chardonnay*
RED: *Triune*

KAUTZ VINEYARDS AND WINERY
SIX MILE ROAD
P.O. BOX 2263
MURPHYS, CA 95247
(209) 728-1251

HOURS: *11 a.m.–4:30 p.m. daily*
TASTINGS: *Yes*
CHARGE FOR TASTING: *No*
TOURS: *Yes*
PICNIC AREA: *Yes*
RETAIL SALES: *Yes*

DIRECTIONS: *From Main Street in Murphys, drive south on Algiers Street (next to the Murphys Hotel) and turn right on Six Mile Road. The winery entrance is about one mile south of downtown Murphys.*

STEVENOT WINERY

Murphys

During one of our most recent visits to the Stevenot Winery tasting room, considerable attention was being attracted by a dramatic photo display showing a raging forest fire licking at the vineyards. Only weeks before, the popular winery had miraculously been spared from a summer inferno that roared through thousands of surrounding acres, down the adjacent ridge, and within inches of the Stevenot buildings and vines.

In fact, some of the Murphys locals I talked to believe the brave stand taken by firefighters at the winery turned the savage blaze on a

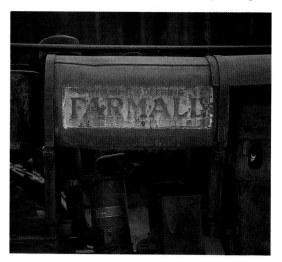

course away from town. Had it continued unchecked, the historic burg might also have burned.

In addition to being remembered as "the winery that saved Murphys," Stevenot (the second *t* is silent) has come to be regarded as the winery that put the Calaveras County region on the wine map.

Since 1974, when Barden Stevenot planted his first grapes here at an elevation of nearly two thousand feet, the establishment has won hundreds of medals for a collection that now stands at some ten wines. (Incidentally, Stevenot vintner Chuck Hovey is also the winemaker at Chatom Vineyards; see separate listing.)

The 160-acre Stevenot estate is sprinkled with a mix of old and new buildings, including a hundred-year-old barn in which a man was reputedly hanged long ago. When things go awry here, workers blame the man's ghost, which some say haunts the place.

The Stevenot tasting room is unlike any other in California. It's a turn-of-the-century log-walled cellar built into a gentle slope and topped by a growing sod roof. The rustic shelter was built by the original owner, a rancher who after a trip to Alaska set about creating an earth-covered structure typical of those found a hundred years ago in the land of the midnight sun. At one time, Alaska House, as it's known, was the hideaway of a convicted murderer on the lam.

Despite the drama that's been played out here over the years, things are usually quiet in this little valley. Trellis-covered tables and a lush lawn provide one of the nicer picnic spots in the foothills, and chilled bottles of Chardonnay and White Zinfandel are only steps away.

THE WINE LIST

Chardonnay Reserve
California Chardonnay
Chenin Blanc
White Zinfandel
Merlot Reserve
Cabernet Sauvignon Reserve
California Cabernet Sauvignon
Zinfandel Reserve
California Zinfandel
Late Harvest Zinfandel
Late Harvest Muscat

VINTNER'S CHOICES

WHITE: *Chardonnay Grand
    Reserve*
RED: *Cabernet Sauvignon
    Grand Reserve*

STEVENOT WINERY
2690 SAN DOMINGO ROAD
MURPHYS, CA 95247
(209) 728-3436

HOURS: *10 a.m.–5 p.m. daily*
TASTINGS: *Yes*
CHARGE FOR TASTING: *No*
TOURS: *By appointment*
PICNIC AREA: *Yes*
RETAIL SALES: *Yes*

DIRECTIONS: *From downtown Murphys, drive north on Sheep Ranch Road and turn right at the entrance to Mercer Caverns. Turn left on San Domingo Road and follow to winery, one mile beyond Mercer Caverns.*

A GUIDE TO NONTRADITIONAL WINES OF THE BACK ROADS

On any backroad winery tour, you'll find plenty of the famous fine varietals that have placed California on the wine map. But along with Cabernet and Chardonnay, you'll encounter wine lists with less familiar names, like Roussanne, Trebbiano, Malbec, Pinot Gris, and Sangiovese.

On California's back roads we met a number of vintners who are stepping outside traditional enological boundaries by working with grapes rarely — if ever — used by other Golden State winemakers. Since Northern California's maverick vintners represent the driving force behind this trend, tasters willing to bring something new and different home to the dinner table will discover some true finds.

Just so you're not tasting in the dark, the following is a brief listing of a few grapes whose names may be unfamiliar to some.

ALEATICO
See Sangiovese

MALVASIA
The white Malvasia is commonly used as a blending grape in Chianti made in Italy's Tuscany region. Fortino Winery of Gilroy describes Malvasia as the "famous ancient grape of love originated from the island of Sicily."

MARSANNE
Bonny Doon Vineyard's Randall Grahm likened one of his Marsanne crops to "marzipan, almond blossom, and honey."

MOURVEDRE
Mourvedre, popular in France, has only recently been rediscovered by California winemakers. Bonny Doon's Grahm, who markets his Mourvedre as Old Telegram, describes the wine as loaded with blackberry and anise.

MUSCAT CANELLI
This grape, sometimes referred to as Muscat Blanc or Muscat Frontignan, makes a sweet white dessert wine that is gaining in popularity. Backroad wineries offering this include Sobon Estate, Perry Creek Vineyards, and Kirigin Cellars. Try it alone as an aperitif or pour it over a bowl of melons.

NEBBIOLO
See Sangiovese

PETIT VERDOT
Bordeaux winemakers commonly use this grape in blending; a few California backroad wineries have begun to incorporate it in Cabernet Sauvignon.

PINOT BLANC
You'll notice the similarity of this wine to Chardonnay; Pinot Blanc has a more subtle, tart taste.

PINOT GRIS
Elliston Vineyards in Sunol maintains one of the state's only plantings of this spicy grape, which makes a full-bodied white wine. Elliston uses Pinot Gris in a special blend.

ROUSSANNE
Roussanne, often blended with Marsanne, is finding its way into white California wines made in the style of the Rhône region of France.

SANGIOVESE
This is the primary red variety of Italy's famous northern Chianti district. Monteviña Winery in Plymouth is devoting close to one hundred acres to classic Italian grapes like Sangiovese, Nebbiolo (from which Italian Barolo and Barbaresco wines are made), and Aleatico (a Southern Italian grape). Chatom Vineyards in Murphys also grows Sangiovese.

SEMILLON
Traditionally blended with Sauvignon Blanc as a softener, this white grape produces a light and fruity wine that's being produced on its own by a growing number of vintners, including Fenestra Winery in Livermore.

WINE ROAD RESOURCES

Romantic Inns and Small Hotels

MENDOCINO REGION

Albion River Inn
3790 North Highway 1
Albion, CA
(707) 937-1919

Glendeven
8221 North Highway 1
Little River, CA
(707) 937-0083

SONOMA REGION

Madrona Manor
1001 Westside Road
Healdsburg, CA
(707) 433-4231

Applewood: An Estate Inn
13555 Highway 116
(Near Guerneville)
Pocket Canyon, CA
(707) 869-9093

Kenwood Inn
10400 Sonoma Highway
Kenwood, CA
(707) 833-1293

NAPA REGION

Meadowood Resort Hotel
900 Meadowood Lane
St. Helena, CA
(707) 963-3646

Wine Country Inn
1152 Lodi Lane
St. Helena, CA
(707) 963-7077

The Elm House
800 California Boulevard
Napa, CA
(707) 255-1831

CENTRAL COAST REGION

Babbling Brook Inn
1025 Laurel Street
Santa Cruz, CA
(408) 427-2437

Inn at Depot Hill
250 Monterey Ave.
Capitola, CA
(408) 462-3376

SIERRA FOOTHILLS REGION

Dunbar House, 1880
271 Jones Street
Murphys, CA
(209) 728-2897

Gold Quartz Inn
15 Bryson Drive
Sutter Creek, CA
(209) 267-9155

The Foxes in Sutter Creek
77 Main Street
Sutter Creek, CA
(209) 267-5882

Recommended Restaurants

MENDOCINO COUNTY REGION

Boonville Hotel
14040 Highway 128
Boonville, CA
(707) 895-2210

SONOMA COUNTY REGION

Della Santina
101 East Napa Street
Sonoma, CA
(707) 935-0576

Glen Ellen Inn
13670 Arnold Drive
Glen Ellen, CA
(707) 996-6409

Cafe Citti
9049 Sonoma Highway
Kenwood, CA
(707) 833-2690

NAPA COUNTY REGION

Tra Vigne
Highway 29 at Carter Oak
St. Helena, CA
(707) 963-4444

Terra
1345 Railroad Ave.
St. Helena, CA
(707) 963-8931

Mustard's Grill
7399 Highway 29
Yountville, CA
(707) 944-2424

The French Laundry
Webber Avenue at Creek
Street
Yountville, CA
(707) 944-2380

CENTRAL COAST REGION

Casablanca
101 Main Street
Santa Cruz, CA
(408) 426-9063

Shadowbrook Restaurant
1750 Wharf Road
Capitola, CA
(408) 475-1511

EAST BAY REGION

Wente Brothers Sparkling
Wine Cellars Restaurant
5050 Arroyo Road
Livermore, CA
(510) 447-3696

Mrs. Coffee and Bistro
Nob Hill Shopping Center
3004 Pacific Avenue
Livermore, CA
(510) 449-1988

SIERRA FOOTHILLS

Imperial Hotel
14202 Highway 49
Amador City, CA
(209) 267-9172

Pelargonium
51 Hanford Street
Sutter Creek, CA
(209) 267-5008

Ruby Tuesday
Eureka Street Courtyard
Sutter Creek, CA
(209) 267-0556

PRIMO PICNIC PLACES

Following, by region, are wineries whose picnic areas are highly recommended by the author. All have picnic tables. We suggest (and some establishments stipulate) that you follow backroad winery etiquette and not open wine from another winery during your picnic. These picnic areas are for winery visitors only. Most sell chilled wines. Refer to winery entries for directions.

MENDOCINO COUNTY REGION

Greenwood Ridge Vineyards — vineyard and water views

Husch — vineyard and local views

Handley Cellars — patio with vineyard views and sculptures

EAST BAY REGION

Concannon Vineyard — vineyard views

Retzlaff Vineyards — ranch and vineyard views

SONOMA COUNTY REGION

Gundlach-Bundschu Winery — vineyard and winery views

Mill Creek Winery — deck at top of trail; panoramic valley views

Field Stone Winery — oak-shaded tables; foothill and vineyard views

NAPA VALLEY REGION

Château Montelena — reservations required; lake and vineyard views

Vichon Winery, 1595 Oakville Grade, Oakville (not listed in book) — register at winery; panoramic vineyard views

Château Potelle — call ahead; vineyard and panoramic mountain views

COASTAL MOUNTAINS

Sunrise Winery — ranch setting

Ridge Vineyards — spectacular valley views

Hallcrest Vineyards — vineyard views

SIERRA FOOTHILLS

Story Vineyard — panoramic valley, foothill, and mountain views

Boeger Winery — secluded setting

Fitzpatrick Winery — panoramic foothill and mountain views

Monteviña Wines — vineyard views

Stevenot Winery — vineyard and valley views

BACKROAD WINE TOUR MAPS

Free road maps that include updated regional listings of wineries, along with hours and services, are available from the following vintner organizations, or at tasting rooms of member wineries:

Santa Cruz Winegrowers
P.O. Box 3222
Santa Cruz, CA 95063
(408) 458-5030

Santa Clara Valley Wine
Growers Association
P.O. Box 1192
Morgan Hill, CA 95037
(408) 779-2145 or 778-1555

Amador Vintners Association
P.O. Box 596
Jackson, CA 95642
(209) 223-0350

El Dorado Wine Grape
Growers Association
P.O Box 248
Placerville, CA 95667
(916) 622-8094

Livermore Valley Winegrowers
Association
P.O. Box 2052
Livermore, CA 94551

Calaveras Wine Association
c/o the Calaveras Lodging
and Visitors Association
P.O. Box 637
Angels Camp, CA 95222
Toll free: (800) 999-9039;
when call is answered, press
0 to request a map from the
office staff.

Index